ANXIETY
AFTER
CANCER

How Beating Cancer Makes Life Worse
(And How to Turn It Around)

ANXIETY
AFTER
CANCER

How Beating Cancer Makes Life Worse
(And How to Turn It Around)

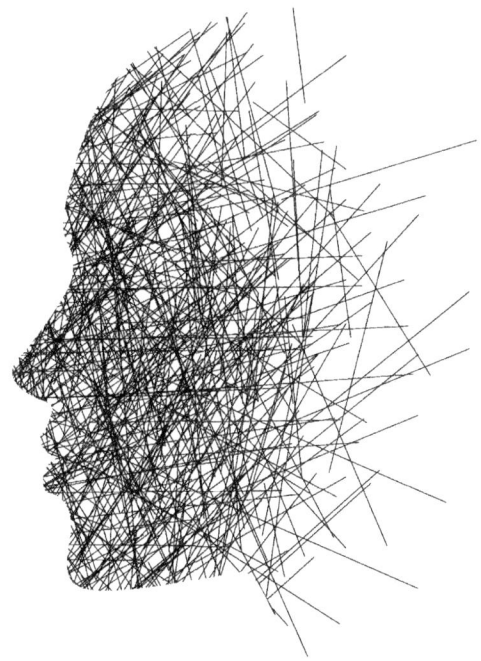

B.H. LINDBLAD

This book contains advice and information related to health care.
It should be used as a supplement rather than replace the advice
of your doctor or another trained health professional.
If you know or suspect you have a health problem,
it is recommended that you seek a physician's advice
before embarking on any medical program or treatment.
The publisher and author disclaim liability for any medical
outcomes that may occur as a result of applying the
methods suggested in this book.

Interior designed by Rebecca A. Stone

Copyright © 2019 by Bradley H. Lindblad
All rights reserved.

To Jacey and my parents

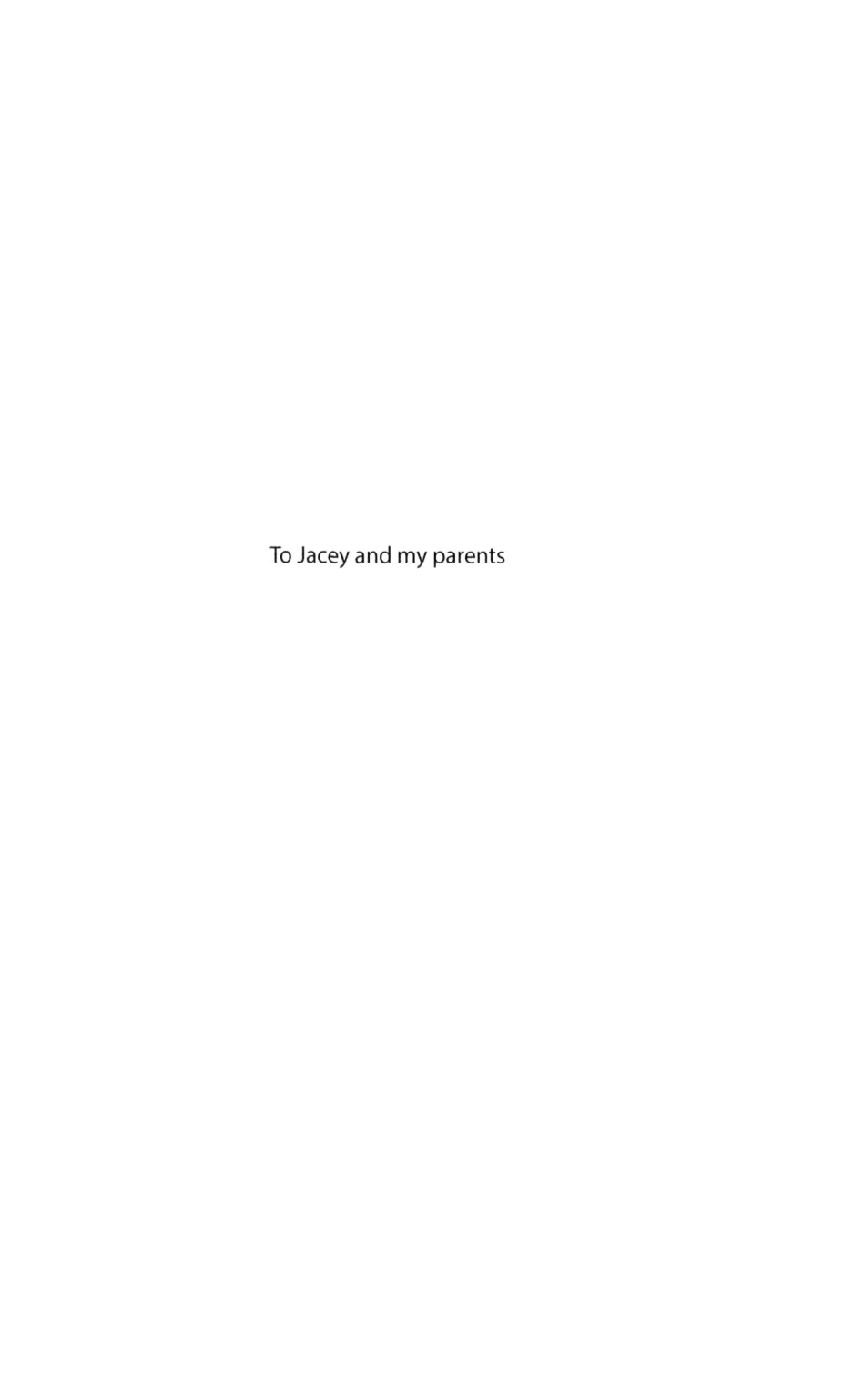

CONTENTS

PROLOGUE 9

PART I: The Thirst of Samson 13

INTRODUCTION 15

CHAPTER 1: Anxiety, or That Fear Gremlin 19

CHAPTER 2: PTSD, or the 1000-Yard Stare 29

CHAPTER 3: Cancer Fears 39

CHAPTER 4: Panic 47

PART II: Facing the Lion 55

CHAPTER 5: Have a Tingle Orgasm 57

CHAPTER 6: Train Yourself Like a Puppy 61

CHAPTER 7: Undo Chemo Fog 75

CHAPTER 8: Sweat it Out 79

CHAPTER 9: Focus on Art 83

CHAPTER 10: Heal Your Gut ··· 89

CHAPTER 11: Try Music Therapy ······································· 93

CHAPTER 12: Meditate and Change Your Brain ··············· 97

CHAPTER 13: Freeze the Anxiety Out ······························ 101

CHAPTER 14: Drink Matcha Tea ······································· 107

CHAPTER 15: Your New Favorite Spice ···························· 113

CHAPTER 16: Pump Up That Testosterone ····················· 119

CHAPTER 17: Breathe Like a Navy Seal ···························· 127

CHAPTER 18: Try Acupuncture ··· 133

CHAPTER 19: Give Your Worries Away ····························· 137

PART III: The Honey ··· 145

CHAPTER 20: Growing From Cancer ································· 147

CHAPTER 21: Taking the Final Steps ································· 153

BIBLIOGRAPHY ··· 155

PROLOGUE

"One day's happiness makes a man forget his misfortune;
and one day's misfortune makes him forget his past happiness,"
— Ecclesiasticus

A BLACK SWAN

I woke up on February 6, 2012 as one person and ended the day as another. I went from being an invincible twenty-three-year-old business school grad with a penchant for partying to damaged goods.

It started after my 4:00 a.m. shift was over. I went to the orthopedic surgeon's office to get the stitches removed from my surgery a few weeks prior. The surgeon removed a wart that had been in the palm of my left hand for close to a decade. I remember walking into the doctor's office in my filthy blue jeans, Merrell fleece, and brown Fox Racing cap, feeling underdressed and decidedly blue-collar.

As I waited for the surgeon to come in, I thought about my agenda for that evening; the big decision on my plate was whether to go hot-tubbing or not, knowing full well I would only get a few hours of sleep before my next shift began. The surgeon stormed in the room and interrupted my thoughts, a look of fear in his eyes, like a raccoon in a trap. As the words oozed from his mouth, scenes from TV shows depicting this scenario flitted across my mind's eye, probably like one's life flashes before their eyes at death. Being on the receiving end of a cancer diagnosis was surreal. It's something that happens to the other guy, not me. Not at my age.

I plodded to my pickup truck. Some of the more salient points the doctor made ran through my head: "If I were you, I'd go to a regional specialist, like Mayo in Rochester or Sloan in New York…the pathologist has never seen a cancer like this one before…this cancer can be especially dangerous…it depends how far it's spread."

Fuuuck. Just as I had the world by the haunches, fresh out of school, ready to make my mark, I get sideswiped by this. This, this cancer. What the hell is cancer, anyway? Just some tumor or something? How could that kill you? Can't they just cut it out and be done with it? I wasn't meant to rest upon a throne of invincibility in my twenties, like most people, which made me furious.

I went to my parents' house to break the news and get some parental reassurance. I sat down in the recliner—the same recliner I sat in as a child to get asthma medicine when I couldn't breathe—and worked up the courage to tell them what I had become. I spit the words out and didn't wait to see their reactions; it was too much to handle. Then I called my grandparents, then my sister. It was harder to tell my family about it than to hear the news myself.

I came home to find my roommate playing the latest *Call of Duty* game on XBox, *Modern Warfare 3,* which we both agreed was nowhere near as awesome as its predecessor, *Modern Warfare 2*. He took the revelation calmly on the outside, but I felt his youthful invincibility projected onto me, both for my support and his. "You're young, you'll beat this. It can't be that bad if it's in your hand…"

After my traumatic initial diagnosis, I had a battery of tests including MRIs, CAT scans, and PET scans. Later that week I had a blind date set up at a bar in the neighborhood. That evening, I went to my parents' to get some supper before the date and to freshen up after a workout. I also did something that I had never done before: a cosmetic face mask—something to give me that extra boost I needed to hit it off well with my new tryst. Something to hide the cancer in me. Something whispered to me that this was my last chance to look normal enough to attract a mate; I needed to pull out all the stops to look my best. No one would want to date or marry someone who looked like a balding charity case.

A friend from work had set up the date. She was a blonde with ruddy cheeks and legs enveloped in knee-high boots. It was my first blind date ever, and I wasn't sure what to expect. Luckily, our mutual friend had laid the perfect groundwork between us to spark quick chemistry. My hand was healed from my first surgery at this point, so there was nothing that could have led her to believe that I was anything but a healthy twenty-something like every other guy on the market. At some point, the conversation led to the Panera Bread restaurants and my complete ignorance to their existence. This Nordic *kvinna* was from the Minneapolis area and grew up infatuated with the overpriced sandwiches and pastries, and she decided she needed to bring me a little bowl of Panera potato soup she had cached in her freezer like some sort of blonde squirrel.

This was my first glimpse into the character of this girl. I knew that I would probably need some serious help in the near future, so this obvious signal of the nurturing instinct was more attractive to me than the tightest of yoga pants. Through the next nine months, she wouldn't leave my side, displaying superhuman care, altruism, and love. If falling in love is the best feeling in the world, then it's the perfect foil for the worst thing in the world. The blind date was a welcome distraction in a surreal week. The next morning, I had to confront the cancer beast again. At that point, it seemed like I might get off easy. There was a chance that the cancer was contained to my hand, and that all I would need was local radiation and maybe some light chemo for good measure. Hopefully.

PART I

THE THIRST OF SAMSON

Samson dropped the donkey's jawbone and laid his head against a limestone rock. He started to weep, pitifully, like a child. He had dispatched dozens of Philistines by himself, but now the hot Judean sun beat mercilessly on his brow. His muscles twitched with exhaustion. He had summoned superhuman strength and faced an entire regiment of the enemy, but now, he thirsted.

The thirst was unbearable—so much so that he began to envy the dead littering the barren landscape. He gazed despondently at the heavens and cried, "You have accomplished this great victory by the strength of your servant. Must now I die of thirst and fall into the hands of these pagans?"

Even though he had done something that no one before him had dreamed of, he cried out in his thirst. His want of drink weighed more heavily on his soul than the seemingly impossible task he had accomplished.

To most people reading the story of Samson, it may seem odd that the powerful Judge of Israel would lament a relatively insignificant setback. Yet, the real challenges of this life are not the ones we expect. As Nassim Taleb notes in *The Black Swan*, "the payoff of human venture is, in general, inversely proportional to what it is expected to be." While we may believe beforehand that cancer will be the most painful thing to ever happen to us—and at that point, it probably is—this just isn't always the case. The thing that is worse is the Black Swan—the unexpected yet profoundly impactful thing that changes our lives the most. It affected Samson, and if you're reading this, it probably affected you too.

INTRODUCTION

It came suddenly after nearly a decade of silent infiltration. As a child, doctors told me that the small bump on the palm of my left hand was a wart and that it would eventually go away, and that I should worry less and quit being so neurotic. Well, it didn't go away, and when I eventually had it removed when I was twenty-two years old, they told me that that "wart" was a rare form of cancer called sarcoma.

Five surgeries and nine months of chemotherapy later, I beat the cancer, or so I thought. All my friends and family congratulated me on the big W, which further convinced me that I had indeed won the battle. But, I didn't feel like I had won. The trauma of the fight had quietly sown the seeds of discontent in my soul. These seeds have a pernicious tendency to germinate and grow under our skin where we can't readily observe. When the fully-formed monster does reveal itself, it can often be too strong to fight with conventional weapons.

NOTHING NEW UNDER THE SUN

Cancer survivors often find themselves in the same predicament that Samson did so long ago. We beat cancer, think everything will be okay, then get saddled with the emotional equivalent of a millstone around our necks. We look forward to the last day of treatment as much as we looked forward to the last day of school; we can't wait to be done with that BS. Two months after graduation, however, we realized that life isn't as easy as we thought it would be. There are bills to pay, 401(k)s to fund, responsibilities to own. After cancer is in your rearview mirror, your mind starts to wander. Certain doubts emerge, quietly at first.

What if it comes back? What if my radiation site is sore like this forever? What if this is all a joke and the cancer spread, but the doctor doesn't see it yet? What if I get nauseous at the sight of lettuce for the rest of my life?

But, we are free now. Free from white blood cell counts, free from wearing wigs and face masks to the mall, free from hurting all over. But then these pesky "what-ifs" start to creep in. Like Samson, we are torn down by these seemingly insignificant troubles after we think our fight is over. But our fight isn't over yet—it's just beginning.

I lived this reality for more than a year. I trembled through my days with worry and angst. The anxiety came out of nowhere, and in short order I was enveloped in a paralyzing state of fear and dread. All the emotions I had been repressing about my cancer experience had finally surfaced, no longer submerged in the mental slough that I hadn't cared to visit. I was always afraid. I dreaded bedtime, the only time of day when I couldn't distract myself from these thoughts—thoughts of relapse, thoughts of being sent to an early grave by the disease I thought I'd beaten. I couldn't drive by a medical facility without gagging at the memory of horrific days in the chemo chair.

What I was experiencing was acute anxiety and post-traumatic stress disorder (PTSD). At my lowest point, I took the onus upon myself to research how I could get over this and get on with my life. I read everything I could: books, blogs, medical journal articles, and all flavors of internet. I learned that I wasn't alone. More than 50 percent of cancer survivors experience acute anxiety at some point after beating cancer. More importantly, I learned that I was, in fact, not crazy, which was my biggest fear by far.

After applying all my research and self-experimentation for months, I eliminated 90 percent of my anxiety and depression symptoms, turning my life around in the process. This book will give you the keys to my success. You'll learn more than a dozen safe, natural weapons you can use to slay the monster that cancer birthed in your life. Things will get better. You will be empowered to fight the anxiety and depression that's getting in the way of your happiness and peace. Armed to the teeth with these techniques, you will bristle with confidence as you take back control and enjoy the gift that comes with cancer survivorship.

How to use this book

This book is divided into three parts: Part I breaks down precisely how and why survivors are afflicted with anxiety after defeating cancer. Part II gives you the tools you can use to fight anxiety and depression, and Part III shows you how to gather the spoils of victory and strut away from cancer better than you started.

Disclaimer

I am not a doctor. You should probably run these tactics by your physician before trying them, even though they are perfectly safe. I am simply a cancer survivor sharing a few things I learned, so be responsible, and talk to real experts, too.

CHAPTER 1

ANXIETY, OR THAT FEAR GREMLIN

"On all the peaks lies peace." — Goethe

"Happiness is not a brilliant climax to years of grim struggle and anxiety. It is a long succession of little decisions simply to be happy in the moment."
— J. Donald Walters

I ease the Chevy Malibu into the parking garage next to the oncologist's office. I'm blinded for a few seconds as my eyes adjust to the cavelike interior after being out in the oppressive midsummer sunlight. Already, my fingers are tingling, my mouth is like Death Valley, and my heart rate climbs past fat-burning zone into peak-intensity zone. I feel the seat belt pressing into the spot on my chest where my port was removed a few weeks ago, still sore. I unbuckle myself, working up the guts to open the door and face the music.

It gets worse. My heartbeat is now at hummingbird speed. I feel a suffocation feeling deep in my chest. *What if this chest tightness is lung cancer? Wow, get ahold of yourself! Are you listening to what you're thinking?*

The panic intensifies.

If you drive away right now, you'll never have to know if your cancer came back or not. The rationalizations start trickling in. Every night for the last week I'd slept poorly, dreams of my upcoming checkup with the oncologist flooding my mind. I saw myself sitting in the cold white appointment room where I was diagnosed only a year prior. The dreams were very bright, almost like a pleasant, heavenly dream. At the end of each of these episodes, a doctor appeared and his mouth moved, but no sound came out. But in the dream I know what he's saying. I just don't want to hear it.

I had a macho attitude when I was actively fighting cancer. I took great pride in letting the chemo roll off my back like water off a wood duck. I would brag about how I'd be at my desk bright and early Monday morning after a grueling Friday chemo session.

Today, it's hard to feel macho when I can't even walk into the damn building where I took my treatments for the better part of nine months, every Friday morning at seven bells. I can't even open the damn car door.

ANXIETY, OR THE FEAR OF FEAR

What I was experiencing is officially known as "acute anxiety." If you were to look this up on a medical website, you would find a definition like this:

> *"Anxiety is a chronic condition characterized by an excessive persistent sense of apprehension, with physical symptoms such as sweating, palpitation and feelings of stress."*

Common anxiety symptoms include:

- Uncontrolled worry

- Trouble solving problems and focusing thoughts

- Muscle tension

- Trembling and shaking

- Dry mouth

- Restlessness

- Angry outbursts and irritability

These symptoms can manifest themselves frequently in those suffering from anxiety. Some people may only experience a few symptoms such as restlessness and irritability, while many find themselves in a living hell consisting of a nightmarish blend of dozens of these symptoms. Many survivors fall victim to this trap. The initial symptoms are vague enough to ignore or write off, and before they know it, they are drowning in more severe anxiety.

Some of the more intense anxiety symptoms include:

- Intense dread

- Suffocation

- Chills

- Sweating

- Dizziness

- Abdominal pain

- Nausea, indigestion

- High blood pressure

These symptoms are on the extreme end of the anxiety spectrum and are usually associated with panic attacks, which a friend of mine accurately describes as, "the feeling of dying without the relief of actually being dead."

LINKS TO CANCER TREATMENT

> *"If being methodically poisoned with a cocktail of drugs that are designed to kill your very cells or having Hiroshima-esque radiation pounded through your body isn't enough to put you on edge, then maybe the fear of having to do it again will."*
>
> —Anonymous cancer patient

Cancer treatments such as chemotherapy, radiation and immunotherapy affect the human body in many ways. There are obvious side effects such as hair loss, brain fog, and digestive issues, as well as changes in brain chemistry. These changes in brain chemistry may be part of the reason mental issues such as anxiety and depression are so common.

One study found that 27 percent of cancer survivors experience anxiety immediately after treatment. Even more discouraging, the same study found that more than 50 percent of survivors were likely to experience anxiety at some point in the ten years following treatment. You may or may not have heard that the odds that any one person will get cancer in their lifetime is one in three. The current population of the United States as of 2019 was around 330 million. One-third of that is 110 million, and half of that is 55 million. That's a staggering amount of people! To say that post-cancer anxiety is a large problem is a serious understatement.

A study found that anxiety is often overlooked by medical professionals after cancer treatment ends. This may be due in part to a closer focus on depressive symptoms in the same period, which are less common. Indeed, a study pointed out that, "levels of depression in adult survivors two years or longer after diagnosis are almost identical to adults with no history of cancer." The effects of depression also typically last far less than anxiety (two years versus ten years).

FREEDOM IS ANXIETY

"Anxiety is the realization of freedom and the possibility of choice."

—Søren Kierkegaard

Soren Kierkegaard was a Danish philosopher active in the 19th century. He was known as the "Melancholy Dane," primarily because many of his most famous writings focused on the negative side of the human condition, such as suffering and death. Kierkegaard drew from his personal anxieties and fears for much of his writing, which brings the deep understanding that can come only from experience. Kierkegaard practically defined what the word "anxiety" means to us today. In our modern age of information overload, it is worth exploring what the "sanest man of his generation" had to say on the topic:

> *"Anxiety may be compared to dizziness. He whose eye happens to look down the yawning abyss becomes dizzy. But what is the reason for this? It is just as much in his own eye as in the abyss, for suppose he had not looked down. Hence, his anxiety is the dizziness of freedom."*

He argued that anxiety came from freedom, which seems counterintuitive to those who've been engulfed in the suffocating clutches of the condition.

Present-day English philosopher Alain de Botton picks this thought up where Kierkegaard left them almost two-hundred years prior. In his book *Status Anxiety*, de Botton notes that at no time in human history have we had such a dazzling array of choices to make and such monumental social and economic ladders to climb. A peasant from Germany in the Dark Ages would have little hope of moving up the social ladder, and that very lack of upward mobility was the exact reason why the peasant would face less anxiety than someone living today, where the pressure to rise up from fiefdom is ever-present.

The possibility of upward mobility adds weight to the shoulder yoke of modern life. As we look up at the ivory towers that line the street, we know that we can rise to the top if we work hard enough, and that light-headedness is a great source of our anxiety.

The yawning abyss

When you have cancer you feel trapped. Trapped and imprisoned by radiation or chemo treatments, surgeries, and overprotective family and friends worried about your low white blood cell counts. You don't feel like you're in control of your life. Cancer is running the show.

But then, the magic day comes. You're cancer-free, and something happens. You celebrate, obviously. A natural high sets in that stays with you for months, even years. Something like an extended runner's high. This high was journalled perfectly by a friend of mine who is also a survivor:

"Just got done with my last doctor visit after chemo. Dr. Kafka told me that my hair would be growing back in a month or so, and it would be the fullest and thickest hair I would have in my entire life. I can't wait. I even went out and bought some razors afterwards for when my peach fuzz is replaced with some actual whiskers once more. On the drive to class this afternoon I couldn't help but smile the entire way. I felt so alive. It's really hard to describe. The lilacs were in bloom and created a tunnel of incense that my car darted through. The birds singing in the lindens along the road trumpeted sweet music. The chemo and angst- induced knot in my stomach from the last year had been replaced with utter calm, like a Minnesota lake at twilight. I hope these feelings last forever. The last time I felt this way was when I was in high school and fell in love for the first time; nothing mattered besides the feelings that I was having. A meteor could have landed in my backyard and I still wouldn't have been able to shake the infatuation that had seized my heart. Yes, cancer sucked, but it was almost worth it to experience this feeling of joy, utter and complete joy."

Blaise Pascal said that,

"The greatest philosopher in the world, standing on the brink of a precipice, on the amply wide plank, and convinced by his reason that he was perfectly safe, would be undone by his imagination."

This ephemeral high rests upon a veritable tinder box; it only needs a small spark to become engulfed in the flames of worry. The reader knows this feeling. It's a sweet, fleeting feeling. In the same way that peace hugged Europe between the World Wars, this high is delicate and fragile. It can be easily shattered by the what-ifs. One only needs to examine the stakes to see that the dangers actually haven't all passed when you get the all-clear. Relapse is still, unfortunately, common with certain forms of cancer. So now we get to the heart of the matter, the reason many survivors are engulfed by anxiety at one time or another: the imagination. Imagination as to what could (if however unlikely) happen, these persistent what-ifs.

Our imaginations can be highjacked by these anxiety gremlins from time to time and used against us. Survivors can't help but invite these gremlins in, invite in the possibilities of what could happen.

Wouldn't it be easier to not have an imagination at all then? Easier to be an unimaginative drone? Again, Kierkegaard has words for us. He said, "whoever is educated by possibility is exposed to danger." Those of us who have seen just how much cancer and its treatment can destroy our lives and our families can never un-see that. We've been traumatized.

THE CURSE OF CREATIVITY

Does a well-developed imagination lead to anxiety? Maybe. Imagination and creativity are definitely linked. Many of the world's best artists have had mental health issues—one needs to look no further than Vincent Van Gogh's unfortunate ear or to the long list of musicians who've taken their own lives. Art is the only way they found to express these deep, complex feelings they had. Many artists have recognized the link between creative work and anxiety. T.S. Eliot was overheard saying that anxiety, "is the hand maiden of creativity."

Joyce Carol Oates said, "any creative work is likely to be stressful... the more anxiety the more you feel like you're headed in the right direction." Kierkegaard explained that, "because it's possible to create...one has anxiety."

The point to glean from this is that anxiety isn't always a bad thing. Sure, anxiety can feel like the end of the world, but the fact that you are experiencing it only proves that you possess at least a modicum of inventiveness as well as a vivid imagination. Merriam-Webster's dictionary has an interesting definition for anxiety: "[anxiety is] a feeling of wanting to do something very much."

After I beat cancer I wanted to do many things very much, a second chance to do what I took for granted before I got sick. In Part III of this book, we'll learn ways to use this creative anxiety for good.

CHAPTER 2

PTSD, OR THE 1000-YARD STARE

> *"Many call it the 1000 yard stare and can't realize the pain when PTSD takes us there"*
> —Stanley Victor Paskavich

> *"The day came, when looking back on his camp experience, he can no longer understand how he has endured it all... all his camp experience seems nothing more than a nightmare."*
> —Viktor Frankl

Viktor Frankl survived three concentrations camps during WWII. First Auschwitz, then Dachau, and later a rest camp near the Austrian border. A few years after he was liberated by Allied forces, he wrote a book that has gone on to become one of the most inspirational tomes of the twentieth century. *Man's Search for Meaning* documents his observations on human nature from his time as a prisoner.

One such chilling observation was his ability to predict the death of his fellow prisoners. After someone metaphorically "gave up," it would only be a matter of days before they died. They would often lay in their own filth and stare blankly at the cell wall before passing in short order. This phenomenon has also been observed by oncologists when their cancer patients lose hope.

If one reads through *Man's Search for Meaning* carefully, parallels can be found between the mental aftermath of surviving a concentration camp and a cancer battle. It is worth restating what Frankl said above:

> *"The day came, when looking back on his camp experience, he no longer understood how he endured it all...all his camp experiences seem nothing more than a nightmare. The human mind simply cannot comprehend past horrors that it endured, probably as a self-defense mechanism."*

Frankl was rescued by Allied forces in 1945 and returned to a normal life in Austria. He was educated at the University of Vienna in the 1920's and quickly rose to became one of the most eminent psychiatrists and neurologists in Europe. When Frankl was liberated, it was impossible to imagine that he would ever forget what it was like to be a prisoner. It was all he knew for years. But, he learned that the human mind is always working to protect the body, so it allows itself to forget (read: repress) memories that would have caused self-harm. But only to an extent.

As I write this five years after my time in the chemo chair, I can't reimagine what chemo felt like. The retching, the fear, the pain. Time has softened the impact, and my psyche has buried the rest. I can't appreciate my cancer experience in the same way that a student learning about the Holocaust in high school can't appreciate the horrors of that genocide; it's simply too hard to imagine. The experience is so far removed from normal life.

While Frankl quickly assimilated back into society and rose to prominence in his career, many are not as successful in returning to normal life.

DA NANG VIETNAM, 1968

Roy wipes the acrid sweat out of his eyes and peers up at the hot sun that seems to be perched a few feet above the tree tops. It was at least one-hundred degrees in the shade today—standard weather in southern Vietnam. Roy's an engineer with a US Army unit stationed on a base outside of Da Nang, and in the last week the Viet Cong have blown every bridge on the Song Cu De River, interrupting the Army's supply routes. His job is to fix these bridges and get back in one piece.

He takes out his canteen and takes a long drink of the warm, alkali-flavored water. In the distance near the edge of the rice paddy, he hears a muted plop, and his ears prickle. Within seconds he hears the unmistakable whine of an incoming shell—mortar fire. The shell lands directly on a nearby truck, and it explodes with a shock wave that knocks him off the road and into a mangrove tree. His heart races. His body courses with life-saving adrenaline. He hugs the ground and buries his face in the warm mud.

Fifteen years later in sunny San Diego, Roy is in broadcasting after a few brief stints with local radio in Connecticut and New York. He's enjoyed a steady climb up and into the television world where he landed a spot as a morning anchor on a popular news program. It should be a happy time in his life, but his close friends have started noticing the lines in his face deepening into furrows. Daily nightmares and a steady diet of booze and fear are aging the thirty-five-year-old in observable ways. Most nights he drinks his favorite whiskey, Old Taylor, until the memories leave him. Rocket attacks. Ambushes. The makeup artists at the station have to work hard to hide the bags that line his eyes in the morning. When he left Vietnam a decade ago, he thought he had left all that behind.

The Saturday show is the biggest one of the week. Roy is going over today's talking points backstage. He jokes with stagehands to lighten his mood.

"Five minutes!" the stage announcer yells.

Roy's hands start shaking, trembling, and he enters his dressing room and locks the door. He nervously paces back and forth and begins to hyperventilate. The shallow breaths cut the amount of carbon dioxide in his body, making his fingers tingle and his vision distort—which adds to his growing panic. He crushes down into his chair and reaches into a locked desk drawer for his emergency flask of Old Taylor. Taking a long pull, he feels his breathing return to normal. His "medicine" is taking effect. He takes a deep breath and heads out to the set.

SIOUX FALLS, SD, 2016

Eric has had a rough month. His friend, who went through chemo at the same time he did, had a relapse of lung cancer and passed away. Then he had a false diagnosis at a recent checkup. The nurse said that the blood work had shown an irregularity indicative of leukemia and said they needed to do a bone marrow biopsy immediately. As he was being prepped for the procedure, the doctor came in and told him it was a false alarm, someone hit the wrong button in the lab—he was perfectly fine. The episode has haunted Eric and his family for months.

Even though he's still perfectly healthy, the thought that he could have had a relapse have nearly scared him to death. After all, a good deal of the pain that survivors experience is not actual physical pain from the treatment of a relapse, but mental pain from the fact that cancer once again has invaded their inner sanctum.

Then the panic attacks come. A perfectly normal day is interrupted by irrational terror at the slightest trigger: a whiff of hand sanitizer like the stuff used by his chemo nurses, a drive past any clinic, simply thinking about cancer. The triggers become more and more numerous, and the attacks more unpredictable to the point where he can barely function at work or home.

And then there are the night terrors. As he lies in bed in the state between awake and asleep, he's bombarded by negative thoughts. Thoughts of treatment, life before cancer, and dying. A recurring scene that plays out in his mind's eye is his doctor telling him he has cancer again. A relapse. Sometimes, he seizes up, un able to move a muscle, while perfectly cognizant of everything around him. After what seems like an eternity, he snaps out of it and screams, waking the family.

PTSD

The night terrors, fear, anxiety, and panic felt by both men are all symptoms of post-traumatic stress disorder, or PTSD. PTSD is one of the most under-diagnosed mental issues facing cancer survivors—only 10 percent of survivors reporting symptoms of PTSD get the treatment they need.[1] It's interesting to look back at the different words used to describe what we now call PTSD:

- Napoleonic Wars: Nostalgia

- American Civil War: Soldier's Heart

- World War I: Shell Shock

- World War II: Battle Fatigue

- Vietnam War: Stress-response Syndrome

Veterans of wars have always been susceptible to PTSD; the

labels attached to it have changed over time as well as treatment options. Throughout most of history, psychologists were sure that these conditions were acute, meaning short in duration. It wasn't until the 1980's that psychologists realized that this condition can last for years, and the symptoms can change over time. PTSD finally made it in the DSM (mental disorder handbook) in 1980.

Mayo Clinic defines PTSD as, "A mental health condition triggered by a terrifying event-either experiencing it directly or witnessing it. Symptoms may include flashbacks, nightmares or severe anxiety, as well as uncontrollable thoughts about the event." [2]

The traumatic events that cause PTSD in veterans are obvious, most people don't immediately associate cancer survivors with trauma. However, while Roy was dodging mortar attacks and booby-trapped roads in his nightmares, Eric was dodging saline flushes and white blood cell counts low enough to kill Keith Richards. While death on the battlefield can come in an instant, death from cancer often slowly gallops toward its victim like one of the horsemen of the apocalypse.

The intrusive thoughts Eric was experiencing occur in 16-28 percent of cancer survivors.[1] Any pre-existing mental condition such as anxiety or depression can increase the risk of PTSD by fourteen times.[1] Eric did his best after treatment to forget that he ever had cancer. This can often come back to haunt the unlucky ones that can't outrun or hide from their repressed demons. Suppressing these feelings of worry can increase the duration of PTSD and can increase the intensity of symptoms.[1] Imagine that there is a big plastic pool in your backyard that holds all your negative baggage about cancer. Periodically, you add bad feelings to that pool from a garden hose. As these feelings come up, you immediately hose them into the deep end. If the pool was getting too full because there were too many bad thoughts, you could open the drain to slowly let these feelings out, and they would slowly trickle out.

If, on the other hand, you refuse to drain the pool when it reaches maximum capacity, the pool will break and everything will rush out at once, turning your backyard into mud. When this happens, all it takes is a trigger to set you off. Some common ones are routine checkups with an oncologist, television shows that remind one of treatment and cancer, or even having children and spending time in a hospital. The associations with medical facilities is strong in those who have had to undergo treatment for any length of time.[1]

One rather tricky aspect of post-cancer PTSD is the way that the causes of the stress shift from the memory of the event to unrelated stimuli.[1] For example, Roy was initially disturbed by dreams of his times in Southeast Asia, of battles he was in, and of buddies he lost. By the late 1970's he was becoming irritated by many more things, like knocks on his office door and seemingly inane issues not at all related to his time in the military. This tendency of PTSD to transform over time is one of the reasons it is so underdiagnosed; it is increasingly difficult for medical professionals to connect the cancer experience to current symptoms.

Along with the changing nature of PTSD, the disorder also tends to increase in severity over time. One study of breast cancer survivors found that 13 percent saw increased PTSD symptoms more than one whole year after treatment ended. They had a honeymoon period of one year before the PTSD invaded their lives. This latent tendency can be especially demoralizing to survivors who have beat the disease and have lived relatively stress-free for some time after remission.

THE OTHER VICTIMS

> *"It's not just you that gets cancer, your whole family gets cancer."*
>
> — Anon

Eric's wife was the strong, silent type. She went with him to all his chemo treatments and brain scans. She was the face of calm throughout the storm. Eric found comfort in her enduring strong presence by his side during his fight.

Although his wife appeared to be the picture of contentment, inside she was falling apart. Watching her husband slowly lose his hair, his weight, and his confidence, she became depressed but didn't seek help. She reasoned that Eric was going through enough, and if he knew of her misery it would only compound his, so she suffered in silence. What she didn't know was that her feelings are common for spouses in her position.

This group of care-givers often suffers in silence. They were there for you during treatment, during surgeries, during your food cravings and your sickness. They were parents, husbands, wives, and children; they were friends and coworkers. Many will tell you that it's especially hard to watch a loved one go through cancer when they can't do anything about the outcome. This is especially true for parents of young kids with cancer.

Some survivors dismiss the distress of their loved ones, not intentionally of course, but with the rationalization that, "they didn't have the cancer," which somehow makes their plight seem not as bad as the survivor's. New research has shown that these friends and family suffer from PTSD with an even greater frequency than the survivor.[3] One study of parents of young kids with cancer found that

45 percent of mothers and 32 percent of fathers qualified as having full or partial PTSD after treatment ended.[3] It gets worse. Another study found that five years after remission, 19 percent of mothers and 14 percent of fathers still had symptoms of PTSD.[3]

Many of the symptoms or effects of PTSD on survivors are centered around fear and anxiety. PTSD is a serious condition, and if you suspect that you are affected, be sure to schedule an appointment with your doctor. Part II of this book will provide you with tactics you can use to help fight symptoms of PTSD.

CHAPTER 3

CANCER FEARS

*"To contend with the whole world is comfort,
but to contend with oneself, dreadful."*
—Kierkegaard

Many people are afraid of clowns. Have you ever wondered why? You might initially say that they're "creepy." But what makes a wig and some cheeky makeup creepy? Researchers have found that the face paint conceals facial expressions and emotions on the clown; the brain is afraid because it can't immediately tell if that clown is a threat or not. This threat-scanning is an automatic response that you do all day long—whenever you meet anyone, your mind does this without you knowing.

This response is a self-preservation instinct from the early days of human history, back when you needed to decide if that rustling in the bushes was a lion or a squirrel. This response was vital to human survival then and it still is now, although now it is less important, since lion-avoidance isn't part of most people's everyday life.

Fear is the apprehension of the unknown. Fear sharpens the senses, slows down the body's systems, and releases adrenaline, which prepares the body to either fight or take flight. In the past, the people who had the best response won the most fights and ran away from the most lions, and that highly-developed fear response lived on in the human gene pool. So, if you're afraid often, be of good cheer—you've descended from a long line of survivors!

But unfortunately, your body can also be conditioned to fear stimuli that it naturally wouldn't through a process called classical conditioning. The famous scientist Pavlov introduced us to this phenomenon in the 19th century. Pavlov would ring a bell and feed his dogs immediately after. After repeating this multiple times, the sound of the bell would cause the dogs to instantly salivate; they had become conditioned to associate the sound of the bell with food.

My personal "bell" is the smell of hand sanitizer. I was conditioned during my chemo days by the nurses and doctors who would enter my room and clean their hands with sanitizer before attending to me. My brain soon tied that smell to the inevitable discomfort that would follow. This is a fear response I wasn't born with; it was obviously conditioned through repeated exposure. Many survivors develop unnatural fears like mine during the trauma of cancer. In some people the fear can be managed and compartmentalized—it doesn't affect their lives in a major way, while in others, the fear can be oppressive and lead to general anxiety disorder or similar issues. Fear is related to anxiety the same way a chrysalis is related to a butterfly: one gives way to the other.

CANCER AND FEAR

> *"Death is nothing, but to live defeated is to die every day."*
> —Napoleon Bonaparte

Cancer and fear go together like an all-you-can-eat buffet and indigestion. Cancer is one of the top two killers in the current age, so we have every reason to be afraid of it. We are afraid of it because it can kill us, and it does kill us. But the fear surrounding cancer is often quite different for those who have fought the disease as opposed to those who have not.

I asked hundreds of cancer survivors about the specific fears they had about cancer when they were diagnosed. Many were afraid of the unknown, because they didn't know what to expect. While some oncologists are great about being up-front about possible side effects from cancer treatment, others are not, which leads to painful surprises later. One survivor said, "I was never told anything about chemo brain or other cognitive effects." The slowed brain function during and after chemo can be frustrating to many.

The survivors I polled had different fears after they had defeated their cancers. In many cases, the fear after cancer was much worse than the fear during cancer. One survivor noted that, "the fear chokes...it's a real struggle, one that can paralyze. When it does, I can't eat, focus, remember the peace of the day before because of the plague of today's what if's." After I talked to hundreds of survivors, a few common fears emerged.

Fear Number 1: Relapse

> *"We all live in the past, and through the past are destroyed."*
> —Goethe

"Relapse" is a scary word. It brings with it a whole host of fears: doing chemo again, doing radiation again, being not-cancer-free again. Relapse is by far the most cited fear among survivors. I know it took me a full ten months to fear a relapse, partially because treatment was still fresh in my mind; my new norm was to be sick. As I started to drift farther and farther into normal life, cancer treatment got smaller in my rearview mirror. As it got smaller and I became more accustomed to normalcy, the thought of having to do it all over again became more menacing.

If you're not sure if your head is currently in the sand about relapse fear, check yourself for these common symptoms:

- You attribute slight physical ailments to cancer coming back.

- You are afraid to live a full life.

- You have long-term sleep problems.

- You isolate yourself.

- You eat infrequently. [4]

While any singular symptom doesn't indicate that you or a loved one are in fear of relapse, any number of them together shouldn't be taken lightly.

A study recommends that one of the best ways to cope with this fear is to accept it as a normal part of the healing process. If you can be honest with yourself and recognize that you will be anxious before a checkup, the fear is sapped of some of its power.[4] Things that remind you of cancer and relapse will make you nervous, and running away from that fear will tire you while you have a panic attack. Don't be in denial. You've beat cancer, so surely you can beat this.

Fear Number 2: Collateral Damage

> *"He who fears he shall suffer, already suffers what he fears."*
> —Montaigne

Radiation and chemotherapy beat cancer by destroying fast-growing cells in the body. Unfortunately, chemo doesn't discriminate and can kill healthy cells as well. There are countless lasting side effects from cancer treatment, and listing them is beyond the scope of this book. The sheer amount of collateral damage that chemo and radiation can deal tends to incite deep fear within survivors; many fear that their quality of life has been cut short and that the "damage will catch up with me." While I can neither confirm nor deny those charges, I do know that the fear is real.

While this fear is not unfounded, there are certain ways you can frame this fear to take some of its power away. A friend taught me a mind trick that helps build trust in the resilience of the human body. Yes, cancer can be powerful, but the body's ability to adapt and overcome is much more impressive. Here are a few facts that may help you sleep better at night:

An adult can lose 75 percent of their liver, and it will regrow. Literally, your liver will regrow itself like a sponge or one of the weeds in your backyard.

Many advanced forms of cancer will spread to the lungs. In cases where one lung is removed, the remaining lung will over-inflate itself—essentially doing double duty for its missing buddy.

Contrary to what your kindergarten teacher told you, your fingers don't prune when wet because they are waterlogged or soggy, they prune so they can grip better underwater. How crazy is that?

The human body can undergo incredible stresses that will kill most other animals. Case in point: persistence hunters in Africa.

Hunters have chased down prey such as gazelle and antelope for millennia by literally running them to death. The human body can run for dozens, of miles and its systems adapt for incredible exertion. Most animals cannot regulate their oxygen and body temperatures in the same way. These hunters will find an antelope and chase it down until it dies of heat exhaustion, at which point they collect their meal and probably dramatically chug Powerade like in one of those commercials (kidding).

The human body is amazingly resilient. Let these thoughts cloud out the negative ones when your mind wanders.

Fear Number 3: Leaving Family

This is one of the most persistent fears that many survivors face, myself included. When a survivor or current patient's thoughts drift to death, inevitably they will think about how their family will get by without them. How they will pay the bills? How they will raise the kids? Will they forget you after you're gone? These thoughts leave you utterly helpless; there is nothing you can do to fix a situation when you're among the angels.

I really have no practical advice to counter this fear besides faith—faith that God will provide for the family members like he provided for them before. Something you can do to alleviate this fear is to be there for your family right now, because they're suffering too. A study found that partners of survivors experienced more anxiety post-treatment than actual survivors did. When I learned that I was taken aback. I have been researching cancer and anxiety for five years, and I hadn't a clue about this statistic. My wife never let me in on this, and I sure didn't see the signs in front of me. But I'm also a guy, if it's not painted in red in front of me, will probably miss it.

Another study found that quality of life can be impacted more in partners of survivors than the actual survivors.[5] Depression and general stress levels are all higher with the ones that we love. One of the most troublesome facts is that partners experienced "little post-traumatic growth" following cancer remission so they do not experience the natural high or renewed vigor to change the world that the survivor so often does.[5]

These facts tell us one thing: we need to love our families even harder than we previously thought. Your family hopefully gave you legs to stand on as you were fighting cancer. It's easy for their struggles to fade into the background as you are either thriving or swimming in anxiety or depression. Now that you know, your duty is to love those around you and investigate their feelings. Are they depressed? Are they anxious? Take it upon yourself to find out, and give them the same love and care that they gave you.

You too?

James is energetically pacing back and forth in his messy bedroom. He's been working the early morning shift at a warehouse in town. Going in every morning at four has wreaked havoc on his circadian rhythm, but his usually tired eyes are full of life now.

On the other end of the phone, Wade is equally animated. Wade found out that he had lymphoma just weeks after graduating from college with a degree in finance. His plans of partying hard his first summer were cut short by an ugly face-to-face meeting with his mortality. Speaking with James has him more talkative and upbeat than he has been since his diagnosis.

If the NSA is listening in on the phone call, they would be royally confused: two guys, laughing and joking about the number of times they hurled the previous weekend, poking fun at one another for calling in sick after being destroyed by a session with the infamous "Red Devil" chemo drug. This is bizarre behavior that outsiders don't understand. The two young men have been suffering in their own private bubbles up until now. They were both very young to be diagnosed with cancer and had no friends or acquaintances their age to relate to. C.S. Lewis described this best: "Friendship…is born when one man says to another "What! You too? I thought that no one but myself…"

Great suffering bonds people like nothing else can. Sports teams and fighting units in war have gone through tests and struggles and have depended on each other. This bond or "brotherhood" often lasts for life.

As James and Wade wax philosophical about their common misery, they feel the cathartic release described by Lewis above. Surely if he can handle it, so can I.

A strange thing happens to both the young men the next day: the latent fear that has been simmering in their insides like old pea soup has retreated. Their instant connection was a spiritual and mental release for hordes of bad thoughts that had been renting space in their heads. Over the next few months the two will become close friends—brought together by the most unlikely of circumstances. This connection is the first indication of the good things that can come from cancer.

CHAPTER 4

PANIC

Our dog Oskar loves my wife more than he loves me. If I were hanging from the edge of a cliff by one hand, I'm pretty sure he would lick my fingers until I lost my grip and plunged to my doom. This upsets me for a few reasons, but primarily because I saved his life once.

We were visiting a friend's house, and as we walked from our car to the front door, Oskar was tagging along behind us. Out of nowhere, I noticed a chocolate lab running at top speed right for us. Before I could scoop up our pup, the much bigger dog had Oskar by the neck and was thrashing him about. I tackled the lab like the Crocodile Hunter so Oskar could escape. No doubt Oskar would have been history if I hadn't saved him from the jaws of the much larger dog.

You would think Oskar would have had some gratitude for me after that incident, but he still pretends I don't exist, like the cool kids in high school.

We eventually visited that friend again and brought our dog along—we called ahead to make sure their dog was kenneled. As we walked up to the spot where the incident happened, Oskar proceeded to lose his shit. He whimpered, whined, cried, and jumped on my leg, begging to be picked up. We realized that he had some bad memories tied to the place and was having the puppy equivalent of a situational panic attack, also known as a flashback or PTSD experience.

His brain made a solid connection between that location and intense fear, in much the same way we humans might associate a stretch of road where we got in an accident with pain. The brain does this as a precaution to keep the body alive. It does so in a very unconscious manner, since it is so vital to survival.

DIPPING THE PAW IN

"The only thing we have to fear is fear itself." —Franklin Delano Roosevelt

"The more the panic grows, the more uplifting the image of a man who refuses to bow to the terror." —Ernst Junger, soldier in WWI

Before we can alleviate panic attacks, we need to know exactly what they are. A journal entry of mine will shed some light:

"I was sitting at my desk at work today and something crazy happened. I was just working away, and out of nowhere, my world flipped over, and I almost fell out of my chair. My heart started beating out of my chest like I was being chased by a mountain lion. I stopped by Dave's office and told him I was taking an early lunch, hopped into my car and started driving home. My car turned into a panic room; my throat started tightening, and I had an irresistible urge to escape. When I got as far as Center Street, I had to stop at a red light, and everything escalated. I couldn't wait at that stoplight, so I took off across traffic and sped for home. I began to think about which hospital was closest in case I was having a heart attack or something. It was at that point where I felt like I was disconnected from reality, like when you wake up in a dark room and don't know where you are for a split second, so you freak out."

I later found out that the event that made the room flip over on me was vertigo, which is a common condition stemming from crystals in the inner ear. I had no clue that what I experienced was a panic attack, and I didn't know who to talk to about it. The worst part was that I wondered if I was going insane.

AVOIDANCE

When Oskar was a very young puppy, he picked up a habit that has stayed with him to this day: whenever anyone comes home or visits, he will pick up the nearest toy or shoe or napkin and carry it in his mouth to the new human. While still a cute trick, it also provides us with some insight into how panic perpetuates itself. Some puppy books say that a dog will bring you a "gift" as a token of affection. If we look at this through a scientific lens, we can come to a more accurate conclusion. When Oskar was very young, he must have had a toy in his mouth immediately before receiving affection from a human. His brain associated his having a toy in his mouth with receiving affection. Since pretty much everyone will pet a puppy that is wagging his tail and hamming it up, this pattern was continually reinforced in Oskar until it became second nature.

Alternately, we could say that Oskar fears not receiving affection, so he always brings toys to guests to alleviate this fear. This is the real key. Most people who have had a panic attack fear the next attack and the trigger of the original attack. In my case, the vertigo was my trigger, so I lived my life for the following months in fear of a bout with vertigo and the panic attack that would follow. Sometime after the first attack, I had another round of vertigo, but I calmed myself down somewhat by sipping bottled water very slowly and playing games on my phone—distractions. Because I didn't suffer a full-blown panic attack, my subconscious thought that if I sipped water and played phone games, I would be "safe." It was my version of Oskar's toy.

Another example is situational avoidance. Many survivors fear their oncologists' offices, and many suffer panic attacks during or before checkups. In this case, their trigger is the situation or location that caused the initial panic. Their brain associates the office with panic and danger. Sometimes this association is so strong that the survivor will avoid going to the office or may even avoid driving in the same neighborhood.

This pattern can continue for weeks, months, or even years, and the victim never escapes from panic due to this avoidance and distraction cycle, which is self-perpetuating. The part that turns this into a nasty cycle is the fact that avoiding your fear makes it grow. The unseen enemy is often the scariest, and every time he makes you avoid doing what you want to do, he gains some size.

Many people avoid the triggers or situations that gave them panic attacks in the past without even realizing it. The philosopher Friedrich Nietzsche described the dangers of avoidance succinctly: "The worst sickness of men tends to originate in the sentimental way they try to combat their sicknesses. What seems like an easy cure, in the long run produces something worse than what it's supposed to overcome. Fake consolations always have to be paid for with a general and profound worsening of the original complaint."

Simply put, when you try to tunnel away from your fears, at some point the walls cave in, and you realize you would have been better off not taking the cowardly path.

THE PANIC CYCLE

A single panic attack can set off a chain reaction leading to many symptoms that can last for years. For example: woman has panic attack at doctor's office, woman starts chewing spearmint bubble gum during the attack to distract herself, every time woman thinks of doctor's office she has anxiety, woman chews gum to ease anxiety, anxiety upsets woman's stomach, woman associates upset stomach with anxiety, every time woman has upset stomach, woman gets anxious and chews gum…

This seemingly bizarre cycle can continue to mutate for long periods of time, to the point where you have no clue why you are afraid of inane things. This is one of the reasons panic and anxiety sufferers sometimes think they are "going crazy." The only way to stop this cycle is to disassociate these body symptoms—like pounding heartbeat and indigestion—with anxious and panicky thoughts. In other words, we need to teach our subconscious that these feelings are just an illusion and we are in no danger, because no one has ever died from a panic attack or its symptoms, no matter how real the death feeling is.

FACING FEARS

The number one fear people have about panic attacks is that they will die or go crazy. You can rest assured that this will not happen, and you are perfectly safe no matter what your body is trying to tell you. A main source of the symptoms of a panic attack is hyperventilation, or over-breathing. Hyperventilation can cause a temporary and totally harmless change in blood chemistry that leads to tightness in the chest, tingly fingers or toes, and dizziness or nausea. These feelings only last for a short period of time but can mimic symptoms of stroke or heart attack, further increasing their scariness factor.

One way to quickly overcome your fear of panic attacks is to eliminate the effects hyperventilation has on you...by purposefully hyperventilating. If you are a healthy individual, hyperventilation is very safe (if you have asthma or heart issues, consult a medical professional). By hyperventilating on purpose, you are showing your body that the symptoms you were feeling with panic attacks are harmless, and your body will internalize this and pay less attention to those symptoms when they crop up again.

One thing is for certain: if you do not face your fears and continuously avoid the places or things that gave you panic in the past, they will only grow larger in your mind, and your fear of them will grow. By avoiding these triggers, you are feeding them and allowing them to grow into monsters that never should have been. At this risk of sounding too simplistic, the cure for panic attacks is this: face your fears immediately and constantly until you fear them no more. If you fear nothing, there will be no reason to panic.

I happened to be having lunch with a survivor who confided in me about an incident he had the previous day. He was driving to work and passed the clinic where he went through some grueling radiation therapy. For some reason, he had a panic attack like the one I'd had earlier.

At that point, I knew what he needed to do to stop the panic cycle, so I laid it on him. He needed to get in his car after work that night and drive back and forth past his clinic like a teenager cruising Broadway. He needed to do this until it bored him and whatever association his animal brain had been trying to make earlier in the day would be entirely overwritten before it could become permanent.

Panic can be one of the most debilitating gifts to come from a cancer experience. By getting in front of the panic before it takes hold of you, you will be taking control of your life and courageously attacking your demons before they can get a foothold.

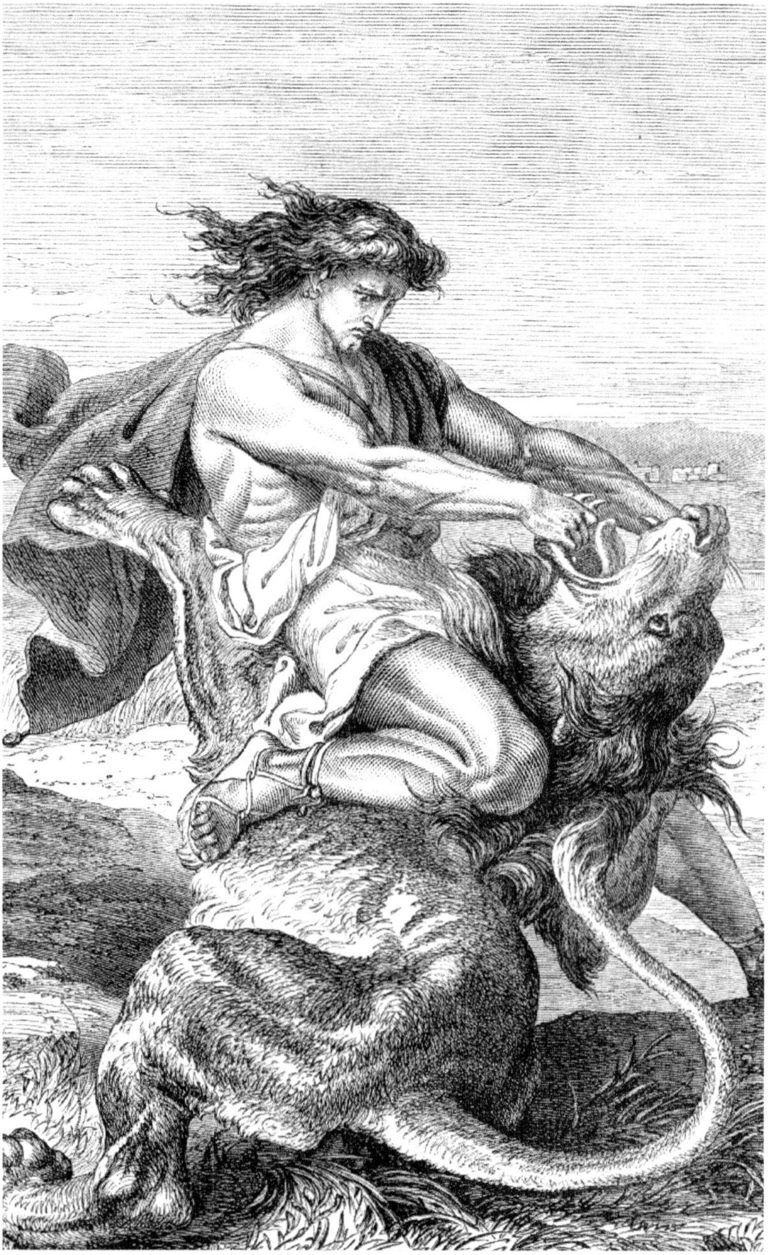

PART II

FACING THE LION

On the roadway near Timnah, in the region of Caanan, Samson came upon an orchard. The grapes were nearly ripe so he took the time to gather a few handfuls for the rest of his journey. The sun was setting, so he picked up the pace to a light jog, trying to make up for lost time.

The sound of his own footfalls masked those of the lion behind him for a bit. Samson barely had time to face the snarling beast before it jumped onto his chest and sank its razor-sharp claws into his pectorals. The two locked eyes, both filled with rage. The acrid odor of the lion's last meal wafted into Samson's nostrils, and he felt like vomiting. Every muscle in Samson's body was 100 percent engaged; he wouldn't be able to hold the beast's head back much longer.

Anxiety can feel like this. Especially anxiety around cancer, its effects on the body, and thoughts of relapse. But we aren't helpless. Like Samson, we may feel like we are small against such a mighty foe, but we do have our cunning, and we do have our brains. We just need to be smarter than the anxiety.

All of the chapters in Part II stand by themselves, so feel free to pick and choose if you like to browse. Each chapter details a real-life tactic you can use to start fighting back against your anxiety. All of the methods herein were tested personally by the author.

CHAPTER 5

GET THE TINGLIES

It was the fourth video conference call that week. The new software was buggier than anyone expected. The developers were working overtime to squash all the bugs, and the client was more than a little bit frustrated.

We all filtered into the meeting room before slugging down our espressos like cattle at a stock tank. I flipped through some time-wasting programs on my phone, wishing I was at my desk getting something done. The lead programmer joined the call; his distinctly Irish accent was still a novelty to us small-town office drones, and we exchanged brief grins before flitting our eyes back to our screens.

My coworker Aaron was up to bat for this call, so he plugged his laptop into the TV system to share his screen with everyone. Then the softest, sultriest feminine voice came over the speakers. His eyes grew huge. I couldn't make out what the woman was saying, but it had a "bedroom" vibe. Aaron scrambled to close the YouTube video he had left open from the night before, wishing he could evaporate out of the room.

Aaron and I were buddies, so I grabbed him after the meeting and asked him as diplomatically as possible, "What the hell was that?" He frantically explained that what I heard was not erotica, but something called ASMR—it relaxes him before bed. I laughed and gave him a hard time but made a mental note to check it out myself.

THE SCIENCE

ASMR stands for "autonomous sensory meridian response," and is a most wonderful sensation that can be hard to explain to those who have never had it.[6] An ASMR experience can feel like "a tingling, static-like sensation across the scalp, back of the neck and at times further areas in response to specific triggering audio and visual stimuli."[7] It appears that not everyone is able to feel the sensation, but those who can feel it usually do before age five—usually from hearing someone talk with an even, monotone voice or from someone gently whispering nearby.[7]

Some who experience intense ASMR describe the sensations as a natural high, while many others say it puts them in a state of "flow," which is a "state of intense focus and diminished awareness of the passage of time that is often associated with optimal performance in activities such as sports." [7] A friend wrote me an email describing his first experience with ASMR:

> *"So that video you sent me was crazy. I've felt that tingling thing on my scalp before, usually when someone is talking in a boring monotone voice. But I never knew how to call up that feeling at-will. I used my nice noise-canceling headphones and put it on right before bed last night. You know those video clips where someone is petting a dog and the dog's kicking like crazy and you know the dog loves it? That's what I felt like. It was awesome. I kind of feel dirty when I listen to it, like I'm doing a new drug that's not illegal yet."*

Testimonials like this are common; 80 percent of people who try it get the "tinglies." The powerful effect on stress and anxiety levels is a bonus feature that we'll exploit.

APPLY IT

If you've never had an ASMR experience, don't worry. Many people can be triggered into having an experience with a little prodding. Some say that you either have it or don't, but realistically those that "have it" more likely have a larger number of triggers. A study has shown that whispering is the most common trigger, with 75 percent of a sample group citing it as a trigger to ASMR.[7] Personal attention such as brushing, combing or massage was the second-most prevalent with 69 percent of a group citing it, and crisp sounds such as crinkling paper or cellophane was also very popular with 64 percent of the sample group picking it as a trigger.[7]

One of the easiest ways to trigger ASMR is to use a scalp massager—one of those little devices that looks like a group of tiny tent poles that envelope the scalp—and gently massage with dozens of tiny round massager points. Buy one and have a friend or significant other gently massage your scalp with it. You should start to feel tingling after a minute or so of stimulation.

Little scientific research has been done in the field of ASMR, partially because there isn't much money to be made from it. There are, however, mountains of anecdotal evidence to corroborate the effectiveness of ASMR for relaxation and stress relief. YouTube has become a gathering place for ASMR enthusiasts. A popular ASMR content creator has more than 300,000 subscribers with millions of views. Many people listen to these YouTube videos with headphones and form a community around the phenomena with comments and discussion. These videos act as a form of guided meditation, with the narrator gently walking the listener through relaxing experiences and sensations. These people also flock to Reddit to discuss; the dedicated subreddit has more 86,000 subscribers. A survey of ASMR enthusiasts showed that 80 percent of listeners use the videos to help fall asleep, and 70 percent use ASMR for stress relief.[7] The same study found that people with high depression levels found the greatest relief from ASMR over the rest.[7]

There aren't many things in life that are both pleasurable and healthy, simultaneously. ASMR is one of those odd exceptions: there is no risk in seeking the experience, and users overwhelmingly leave a session feeling more relaxed, rested, or sleepy, depending on the goal. I personally wish I would have discovered it while I was still going through chemo, because the therapeutic effects would have been a relief. Many have noted that listening to an ASMR video while working can almost immediately put them into the hard-to-find "flow" state that increases productivity.

My friend Aaron begged me to add: under no circumstances, for no reason, should you leave an ASMR session open while hosting a meeting. There's just no decent way to explain it.

CHAPTER 6

TRAIN YOURSELF LIKE A PUPPY

In the 1996 film *Happy Gilmore*, Happy is struggling to concentrate on his golf game, so his mentor, Chubbs, tells him to go to his "happy place, a place in your mind where everything is perfect," and all his anger, "will just disappear." Happy closes his eyes and thinks hard; he imagines himself in a fantasy land and sees his girlfriend bringing him two pitchers of beer, his grandma winning the jackpot in a slot machine, and a small-statured cowboy riding a pony. His idea of paradise. Reinvigorated and de-stressed, he lines up his putt and sinks it.

When I was having chemotherapy sessions, I needed a way to escape—to escape from the pain, to escape from the room and to escape from my own mind. I remembered that scene from *Happy Gilmore* and made my own happy place, except my version involved elements from my own life, like fishing and relaxing on the beach. I could close my eyes and concentrate on this scene and transport myself hundreds of miles away, far away from the cancer clinic and far away from reality.

Unwittingly I had stumbled upon a mental technique called anchoring, where you attach an internal response with some external or internal "trigger," so the desired response can be quickly accessed. Anchoring is a form of neuro-linguistic programming, or NLP. NLP is a powerful suite of mental tools that are by far the most effective tactic in this entire book.

If you want to train yourself to easily find your own happy place, there are a few things you need to know. First, we need to look at what makes up a good anchor (happy place). The anchor:

- must be a unique and specific place or experience

- must be trained as the response peaks

- must be refreshed frequently

These criteria are necessary to train your mind to automatically transport you to your destination. If you think about it, try to remember in detail a mundane Sunday afternoon you had at home where nothing really thrilling happened. It's tough, right? Now try to think of an exciting night out with friends or a fun sporting event you attended. These experiences should come back to you much clearer and more vividly. For our example, let's try to anchor a day at the beach.

Step 1: Recall the State

Sit down in a comfortable chair where you won't be disturbed. Picture yourself lying on a beach somewhere. Get a clear image of what the beach looks like, what the temperature is, and what your surroundings are. This may be difficult depending on the strength of your imagination, but the important thing is to establish the scene in your mind and concentrate on it for several minutes.

Step 2: Intensify Feelings

After you have established the beach environment in your mind, you need make all the sensations much more intense. The trick is to think about the details: how does the sand feel between your toes? Is the sun beating down on your brow? Do you have a cold drink in your hand? What do you smell? If you can attach any particular smell to your experience, you will find that that is the most compelling anchor, because our sense of smell often has the strongest memories attached to it. Think of your dad's aftershave or the smell of your favorite pie fresh out of the oven.

You want to submerge yourself in what your senses would be picking up in this step, almost like stepping into an IMAX theater.

Step 3: Peak the Feelings

Now that we have made our feelings and sensations extremely real, bring these to a peak. Make them ten times more intense. As you do this, squeeze the soft area between your thumb and index finger with two fingers from your other hand. What you are doing is associating this peak experience with this pinching action.

Step 4: Break State

After you anchor the feelings by squeezing your hand, immediately break the state you are in by standing up and walking around or talking to someone—anything to get your mind elsewhere. After a minute or two, test the anchor by squeezing your hand in the same spot as before. Do you immediately think of yourself sitting on a sugar sand beach with a cervesa in your hand? At this point the anchor will be weak, but you should still vaguely recall the beach scene.

Step 5: Lather, Rinse, and Repeat

To firmly establish this anchor in your mind, repeat steps one through four at least ten times. Every day for a week after, you should reinforce the steps to make sure that you never forget it.[8]

ANCHORS FROM CHILDHOOD

The narrator in Marcel Proust's *In Search of Lost Time* explains eating a small sponge cake called a madeline: "No sooner had the warm liquid mixed with the crumbs touched my palate than a shudder ran through me and I stopped, intent upon the extraordinary thing that was happening to me."

The mundane pastry immediately transported him back to his childhood, where his aunt would serve these treats, which he would dunk into hot tea. This is another example of anchoring. We can imagine that these treats were one of the narrator's favorites. Tastes and smells are the two strongest senses available to anchor, and upon tasting the treat for the first time since childhood, the narrator is transported back in time with a rush of emotions and memories. This famous literary example shows how strong an anchor can be, even if it lays dormant for decades.

Find your own

To find your own anchor from childhood, think about something you loved as a child, maybe a treat or candy. For example, in my childhood I would spend time at my grandparents' farm where my grandmother would make me delicious grilled cheese sandwiches. To this day, when I eat a grilled cheese I immediately remember eating my grandmother's, and I remember the house that I ate them in and how it made me feel. One of the reasons this was anchored so specifically was because I never ate grilled cheese anywhere else, so the experience was directly related to that farmhouse.

Once you have thought of a few potential anchors, all that's left to do is to test them out and see if they are strong enough to invoke feelings. In the past, the act of summoning youthful feelings was known as nostalgia, and some psychologists may associate it with regressing to childhood. No matter how you label the phenomena, invoking the spirit of your childhood often brings back great memories and a welcome distraction from anxious or depressing thoughts.

HISTORY OF NLP

Anchoring is a technique that is included in a family of psychoanalytical tools called NLP. NLP practitioners like to say that NLP doesn't work, it explains how you work—perfectly.[9] NLP uses associative and disassociate techniques to change an individual's emotional connections with objects and situations.[10] After several sessions, NLP practitioners can change thoughts and beliefs to eliminate anxious thoughts and bring about a more positive outlook on life.[10] The key to applying these techniques for those suffering from anxiety is to identify the thoughts that are causing the anxiety, which can often be hidden deep within a person's heart. Once those thoughts have been identified, it's only a matter of converting them to more positive ones to find freedom from anxiety.

One of the reasons NLP is so successful for treating anxiety is that it does not cause dependence, while many psychotherapy techniques do cause dependence.[9] NLP teaches patients to think for themselves and to not depend on the therapist for the answers, effectively eliminating any unhealthy ties to the therapy or therapist.[9] A study has shown that NLP can be more effective than prescription drugs in the treatment of anxiety; the study also showed that, "there is little evidence that drugs alone reduce the frequency and severity of anxiety, and afterwards they aren't cured." [9]

How it works

Pink elephant. Try not to think about a pink elephant.

Did you successfully not think of a pink elephant? Probably not. I bet that you even pictured a pink elephant in your mind's eye. It's almost impossible to not picture a thought that comes across your internal stream of consciousness. This amazing feature of our brains is complex and was once necessary for our survival, but now it tends to be more of a nuisance than anything.

Anxiety is a cognitive distortion of this mechanism. In the case of the anxious cancer survivor, it is focusing about what can go wrong—the what if's—rather than what cannot go wrong. It is dreading having a relapse before a cancer checkup rather than meditating on the fact that you will more than likely still be in remission. NLP practitioners call this "sorting for danger," where the patient has become adept at putting the dangers of a situation in the front of their mind and putting all the safeties of a situation in the back.[9]

In a way, anyone suffering from anxiety has learned a skill that would at one time in human history have been extremely useful; anxiety is a learned response to look for danger in situations. But, you know by now that this can be a curse rather than a blessing.[10]

One fun trick that is brand new on the anxiety-reduction front is ABMT, or Attention Bias Modification Training. This method trains your mind to look for the good and pay less attention to the bad. A professor of psychology and neuroscience partnered with computer developers to develop a free app that would allow everybody to experience the life-changing power of ABMT. The result was the phone app called "Personal Zen." In the game, two small sprites pop out of the grass like squirrels—one has a happy face and one has an angry face. You must quickly swipe the trail of the happy sprite and ignore the angry one. This trains your mind not to sort for danger, which helps eliminate one of the root causes of anxiety. The app is free and fun, and it slowly kills the remaining anxiety in your body. Win-win!

JET SET

Sanibel Beach, Fort Myers, Florida

It had been several years since I'd struggled with anxiety. I was lying on a beautiful beach in Florida on my honeymoon. My wife and I had been jet-skiing with dolphins all morning and were killing some time before dinner by scorching our North Dakota-white skin in the hot tropical sun. I rolled onto my back, feeling the hot sand under my toes.

My peaceful vacation was over the next morning. I flew back to North Dakota and my wife stayed behind to attend a work conference. I stared up into the ultramarine sky and took a dramatic gulp as our 747 drifted over the Gulf of Mexico, making its way to the Southwest Florida Regional Airport. The ride in was rough; I hadn't flown since I was a baby and feared being "trapped" on an airplane, so naturally upon takeoff I had a panic attack and suffered through the three-hour flight in silence, distracting myself with iPad games. Now that I was flying back all by my lonesome, my anxiety for the flight home was through the roof.

I pulled up a few videos on YouTube about flight anxiety and eventually landed on a video that described a funny way to trick your panic into subsiding. It involved imagining myself in a movie theater and pretending the flight attendants talked like buffoons. It seemed crazy enough to work, so I made a mental note to practice the technique that night in bed.

Funny movies

After further research, I found that the technique was called Reconsolidation of Traumatic Memories (RTM). As Tony Robbins described it, the goal is to "scratch the record" of the place in your mind where the negative memories are stored. Older folks will remember how a scratch on a vinyl record would stop the music; the goal of RTM is to scratch the record in our brain that associates fear with a stimulus (in my case, fear of flying). When the record is scratched enough, there is simply no connection in the brain to make you fear the situation or thing that you once feared. Here are the steps:

Step 1: Access the trigger stimulus

Briefly imagine the scary stimulus. In my case I thought about being on the airplane and feeling like I was trapped and couldn't escape. Imagine that stimulus for a few moments, and then think about something else to clear your mind.

Step 2: Movie theater

Imagine yourself sitting in a huge movie theater. On the screen your situation is playing out in black in white. As you imagine yourself sitting and watching your scary experience, notice how detached you are from the movie. The experience should lose some of its bite. You feel safe as you watch the movie.

Step 3: Rewind

Go to the end of the movie, and quickly rewind the experience all the way to the beginning in under five seconds. In my case, I imagined myself safely at home after my flight to North Dakota and quickly rewound my flight from end to beginning. Flight attendants walked backward, and the plane landed in reverse back in Florida. Do this several times.

Step 4: Add silliness

Now play the move from beginning to end, still in black and white, but this time add silly music or ridiculous elements to the people around you. Make it as silly as you can imagine. Since I am immature, to this day the 2004 movie *Napoleon Dynamite* still cracks me up. I imagined that the captain had Napoleon's voice, and that the people sitting next to me were other characters from the movie. I added funny music from a circus or carnival, and events unfolded very fast in front of me. I did this dozens of times until I couldn't think about flying without thinking about those funny characters or the funny music. My record was scratched deeply and wouldn't play correctly again.

This technique has been shown to remove intrusive avoidance symptoms (avoiding the cause of anxiety) in 75–85 percent of patients that try it.[11] My flight back home was awesome, my anxiety levels were extremely low, and I even began planning my next trip back to Florida when I got to work the next day.

IN-DEPTH NLP

Dr. Richard Bolstad and Margot Hamblett use the following five-step process to help their patients get rid of their anxiety forever. Their process is deeply rooted in scientific studies and tools that have been proven to instill long-lasting changes in those that use the program. The program consists of:

1. Re-framing anxiety and symptoms

2. Accessing resources and solutions

3. Teaching trance and relaxation anchors

4. Altering sub modalities

5. Creating more integrated beliefs

Step 1: Re-framing anxiety and symptoms

As we discussed in chapter 3, the fear response is a valuable tool that keeps us alive and safe from external threats. By focusing on the importance of fear and anxiety to our survival, we can reframe the anxiety response as a positive element that is necessary to survival.

In the book Magic in Action, the author relates asking a mother who was anxious about her children being out late a few questions. He said, "Let me be you for a day, so if one of your children is late, it will be my job to panic. What do I need inside my head to panic?" This question made the lady think about what reasons she had to panic. She said that she needed to panic because something bad could happen to them. He asked, "So has something bad happened to them before?" to which replied that nothing bad had ever happened. He continued questioning her until she realized that she was really acting incredibly irrationally, and by answering his pointed questions out loud, she came to realize how silly her panic was. Sometimes all we need to do is tell someone else why we are worrying to realize that we are worrying for no reason at all.

At this stage sensory triggers are also re-framed. You may feel tingly fingers when you are anxious, so instead, try to think that your fingers are tingly because you played guitar last night. If you feel faint when anxious, think that perhaps you're not really faint but rather giddy with excitement about something. Replacing a bad feeling with a good one often takes the power of that feeling away immediately.

Step 2: Access solutions

As we discussed earlier, people with anxiety often sort for danger, or bring the danger element of a situation to the forefront and ignore the positive aspects. By accessing the positive outcomes of a situation in the past, you can reinforce the belief that nothing bad will happen. Think about every time something bad didn't happen in a situation—how many times you didn't have a panic attack on a flight or how many times you didn't get bad news at your oncologist's office. It helps to write these affirmations out on paper. Some call it a gratitude journal. Every night write down something you feared that didn't happen. I guarantee you that you can list more positives than negatives.

Step 3: Teaching trance and relaxation anchors

Refer to the beginning of the chapter where we go over anchors and how to set them up. In addition to anchoring, NLP teaches us to relax our bodies systematically. You can do this by sitting comfortably in a chair and starting relaxing your toes. Feel the individual muscles in your feet, and relax them one by one. Don't rush. After your toes are completely relaxed, move up to the muscles in your ankles and do the same thing. Do this from your toes to the top of your scalp, and you should be blissfully relaxed. The magic of this technique is that you can do this in the middle of a crowded meeting and no one will notice.

Step 4: Alter sub modalities

Sub modalities are the building blocks of our memories and thoughts and alter the way we remember or experience thoughts in our brains. While sub modalities are difficult to define and imagine, they are easy to adjust. With their adjustment we can make lasting changes to how we think. One of the most powerful ways to alter sub modalities is to "float above your timeline." For example, let's say we are scared to drive on a particular stretch of highway because of an accident there in the past. To float above our timeline, we need to imagine that we are at our destination. Once you imagine yourself at your destination, try to feel how you would feel at that point: you aren't scared because you drove over that stretch of road and were perfectly safe. Notice how you aren't scared when you look back in time, safe in the future.

For another example, let's take a common scary situation for cancer survivors: follow-up appointments with the oncologist. Sitting in the waiting room waiting to be called into the doctor's office can be nerve-wracking, so try to imagine yourself out in your car after your appointment. How do you feel? Since you had good news at your checkup, you feel totally at ease. Dwell on those feelings and you will find that in the present moment in the waiting room, you also feel fine. It's a great trick that will allow you to celebrate victory before the fight is even over.

Step 5: Create integrated beliefs

Now that we have successfully learned tools to help us re-think and defeat anxiety, we need to consolidate those gains. Realize that the you during an anxiety spell is different from the You at other times. The You on anxiety is irrational and maybe a little bit crazy, while the You the other 90 percent of the time is deeply rational and level-headed. Think about it as almost a split-personality situation. The point is to know that anxious you is separate and distinct from the real You.

NLP is one of the most powerful areas of science that you can learn to help yourself almost immediately. If you apply the techniques that you learn in the chapter and find that they don't help, you should seek out a licensed NLP practitioner in your area for more focused care.

CHAPTER 7

KICK CHEMO FOG

I had always been the first one to hand in my test in high school and college. If I applied myself, I could usually place at the top of the class as well. I was blessed with quick-firing brain cells that retained new information well and retrieved that information efficiently.

After beating cancer, I decided to go to grad school as a personal challenge. Usually, intelligent or ambitious folks attend grad school, which is why I thought I was slightly behind the class. At one time I was able to remember phone numbers and bits of information with ease, but now I was having trouble remembering how to do simple linear algebra that I had once done without trouble. During this frustrating period, a nurse introduced me to the term "chemo brain." She told me that many survivors had foggy memory and reduced cognitive ability after treatment. This naturally hurt me deeply; having a quick brain was how I inflated my ego after a childhood of lackluster athletic performance.

I soon found out that the issue went much deeper than making survivors poor trivia teammates; chemo brain affects many processes essential to good health, and as many as 20-40 percent of survivors complain of cognitive deficits.[12] The most common symptoms are poor episodic memory, slow information processing speed, limited attention span and trouble making calculations.[12] Many of these symptoms don't show up for years after chemotherapy ends, further obscuring the cause of the issues. These cognitive defects are even more pronounced in children who underwent radiation therapy for cancer. These children often had lower IQ scores than their peers, were less likely to attend college, and were even less likely to get married.[13]

Research also hints that jump-starting the neurogenesis process can help ailments such as anxiety and depression. So let's dig in.

THE SCIENCE

Groundbreaking research on these children is beginning to explain why their IQs are lower. Radiation therapy kills cells and chronically suppresses their growth. This suppression of new cell growth starves the brain of materials that it needs to constantly repair itself.[13] This process of making new material, called neurons, is known as neurogenesis.[14] The structure in the brain that produces these neurons is called the hippocampus, and it plays an important role in long-term memory, mood, and emotions.[14]

There are clear links between a decline in neurogenesis and cognitive function and depression; those survivors that had depression often had low levels of neurogenesis.[14] The systemic inflammation that can be present in the body and the brain appears to be the major factor that slows neurogenesis, and indeed radiation and chemotherapy push the body and brain into a highly inflamed state.[13]

Dr. Sandrine Thuret, PhD, is involved in neural stem cell research at King's College in London. She revealed startling information about cancer and neurogenesis in a much-cited TED Talk.16 Dr. Thuret found that much depression in cancer survivors was caused by a deficit in neurogenesis—their brains weren't making the new cells that they needed. She went on to say that there are many things you can do to enhance neurogenesis: have more sex (if you needed a reason), exercise, consume more omega-3 fatty acids, and eat more chocolate and blueberries for their flavonoids. These activities are anti-inflammatory and have an antidepressant effect by supercharging your brain's ability to fix itself and regulate emotions. The most promising of these tactics are exercising and consuming omega-3s.

Exercise

Scientists have known for quite some time that exercise is a useful treatment for mental issues.[13] Exercise has been used for decades to help reverse damage caused by aging and alcoholism.[13] When researchers tested neurogenesis levels in mice that had been irradiated early in life, they found that running was one of the best catalysts to increased brain cell growth.[13] Many doctors already recommend regular exercise for children who had radiation to counter the negative effects on the pulmonary and cardiovascular systems, so this new research provides one more reason to hit the pavement. The next chapter covers the benefits of exercise in more detail.

Omega-3s

Omega-3 fatty acids are commonly found in fish like salmon, trout, and sardines. Many folks consume "fish oil" supplements for heart health. These yellow pills can also be used to combat depression, PTSD, and fear.[15] Studies have shown that intake of dietary omega -3s elevated levels of brain-derived neurotrophic factor (BDNF), which in turn promotes neuronal survival and growth.[15] This means that omega-3s increase neurogenesis, therefore, ease depression and anxiety.

Other studies suggest that intake of omega -3s can minimize the hold that fear can have on our minds.[15] Omega-3s have been shown to clear fear memories from the hippocampus by increasing neurogenesis in the critical window before the memory has taken permanent residence.[15]

In addition to exercise and omega-3 supplementation, Dr. Thuret recommends that patients increase their intake of anti-inflammatory foods and chocolate. Learning is also another activity that can drastically increase the rate of neurogenesis.

While it's easy to feel helpless during a chemo fog episode, you can be assured that there are actionable steps you can take to get your mind sharp again and you should also see your anxiety shrink away.

CHAPTER 8

SWEAT IT OUT

In 2009 Mark Herzlich was named ACC Defensive Player of the Year and was one of the top linebackers in the NFL. During that season he felt a dull pain in his leg. Assuming he had some form of nerve damage or sprain, he went to the team doctor to have an MRI performed. The team doctor referred Mark to an oncologist. If you're reading this book, then you have a pretty good idea of the feeling you get when your doctor refers you to an oncologist. It was then that he learned that he had a rare cancer called sarcoma.

Herzlich was lucky, and his cancer, which typically infects bone, hadn't spread to any other tissue. Seven months of chemotherapy and radiation came next, which left him incapable of training or playing. Although Herlzich had a long recovery from his treatment, he quickly hit the gym and was picked up again as a free agent by the New York Giants. Mark later said, "When I was going through the process, I wouldn't allow myself to fall into that pattern of thinking, 'why me?,' then hope would have been lost. You don't want to lose hope or quit on yourself." Mark found that getting back in the gym was a great mood elevator.

Herzlich's story illustrates how aerobic exercise can be one of the most beneficial activities one can do to normalize oneself after cancer and eliminate anxiety and depression simultaneously. Exercise can be unpleasant, painful, or nauseating for cancer patients and survivors. Chemotherapy and radiation can make the body very weak and can make someone lose tremendous weight or put on large amounts of fat.

Before I had cancer I worked out at least three times every week. I mainly focused on weight training but also mixed it up with cycling, running, and boxing. During chemo and surgeries, I was too weak to do any serious training, and subsequently I put on weight. I began working out one month after finishing treatment and was dismayed to find that I could barely lift the amount that I did as a rank amateur, which was disheartening.

My point is that after treatment for cancer, you will not be in optimal condition, and working out will be stressful at first, both to your body and your ego. It is important to ease into any workout regimen, and check with your doctor first.

THE SCIENCE

Aerobic exercise is viewed by many scholars and medical professionals as *the* most effective way to get rid of anxiety and depression once and for all. The main driver of aerobic exercise's effectiveness is the "feel-good" hormones and endorphins that it releases into the body. Many people describe the feeling that aerobic exercise brings them as a blend of exhilaration and relaxation. Harvard Health explains the technical side of it:

> *"Mental benefits of aerobic exercise have a neurochemical basis. Exercise reduces levels of the body's stress hormones, such as adrenaline and cortisol. It also stimulates the production of endorphins; chemicals in the brain that are the body's natural painkillers and mood elevators."* [17]

The same study also notes some coincidental benefits of adding aerobic exercise to a post-cancer lifestyle: a smaller waist often translates to a more positive self-image, which can reduce overall stress levels. Along with that, the feeling of pride that comes with mastery of a sport such as running or biking can increase one's self-esteem.[17]

An important study of 116 people tested the effects of a twelve-week program of mid-intensity walking for 120 minutes each week. The study participants "exhibited significant improvements in the anxiety levels over time."[18] Researchers went on to point out that "moderate-intensity exercise can be considered an essential component of cancer rehab."[18] Clearly, walking is a low-impact form of activity that should be one of the first things you do to start an exercise regimen after tough cancer treatments.

APPLY IT

There may be more benefits for cancer survivors besides the obvious anxiety reduction and waist-trimming. A study in 2010 recommends that patients and survivors perform an exercise such as biking or walking for twenty to sixty minutes, three to five times per week. They found that this level of exercise not only reduces anxiety, but it improves mood and even reduces fatigue, which can be a lasting after-effect from chemotherapy and radiation treatments.[18]

Based on all these studies, we can say with a good degree of certainty that if you put this book down and go for a walk or a run, you're going to be doing yourself a favor.

But what if you don't struggle with anxiety, and depression is the demon you're trying to slay? Good news: the research that suggests that aerobic exercise eliminating depression is even stronger. Scientists and doctors have noticed for years that their patients who worked out often saw quicker recoveries from their symptoms of depression. Indeed, there are hundreds of studies touting the effectiveness of exercise in decreasing depressive symptoms. Doctors believe that exercise eases depression by reducing immune system chemicals that aggravate depression. Exercise also raises the body temperature, which has a calming effect that soothes the nervous system.

Aerobic exercise is a great distraction: it is hard to feel down when you're maxing out on your long-distance run or sweating buckets thirty minutes into your morning bike ride. Doctors stress that aerobic exercise doesn't necessarily have to be rigorous to provide immense benefits. Gardening, cleaning, and other light chores have been proven to have a beneficial impact on anxiety and depression levels. The Mayo Clinic found that thirty minutes, three to five days per week, was enough exercise to "significantly improve depressive symptoms." [19] While exercise should be one of the first actions to take to rid yourself of your symptoms, it is imperative that you first check with your doctor to be sure exercise is safe for you.

CHAPTER 9

FOCUS ON ART

A large painting hangs on the wall at our family cabin in the lakes country of Minnesota. It is over six feet long and has been in the family for more than fifty years. The artist is an obscure 19th century New England oil painter by the name George Henry Durrie, certainty not one of the most famous painters to come out of that time period but still a dedicated craftsman who captured the heart of rural life in the areas adjacent to his native New Haven, Connecticut. The painting hangs over a long couch and depicts a sprawling farm at the turn of the summer season: pumpkins are stacked in a pile under the eaves, freshly-shucked hay litters the foreground, nebulous mountains rest in the distance. The foreground is painted with rich glazes of ochre and asphaltum paint, trapping the ambient light in several optical layers that forbid the identification of any one color. The sky is opaque scumbles of red lake pigments and lead white, which completes the illusion of space in the composition.

As a young man I thought the painting was amazing in its details. Art class in school taught me that painting should be "fun," and we were encouraged to make Kandinsky-like splashes of random color—really using our paintbrushes like some magician from a children's story. This painting stood in contrast to all that jazz that I really didn't care for, and it romanticized nature in a way that invited anyone to walk right into it.

Spending time in the outdoors exposes me to beautiful scenery and vistas that have introduced me to a new sensation, a sensation and want that I can't easily appease, like hunger or thirst. C.S. Lewis once said that if one found themselves longing for something that had no earthly natural fulfillment—longing for love, sustenance, shelter—then the longing must be for something not of this world. The only explanation, he argued, was that that longing was for something more than we can comprehend with our given minds, a longing for God.[20] He wrote: "We cannot mingle with the splendors we see. But all the leaves of the New Testament are rustling with the rumour that it will not always be so. Some day, God willing, we shall get in...nature is only the first sketch."

Of course, as a child I was unaware of such a theory. I began looking for ways to capture that beauty, a way to bring it with me so I could examine it more back at home—laboriously searching for the Secret. Observing a beautiful scene in the fall beech woods would almost have a frustrating effect on me rather than a calming one: I had to find a way to remember and fully realize this scene now or I would be left unsatisfied like a child who goes to bed without dinner. I started taking hundreds of pictures on a small 35mm camera and building photo albums of all things in nature that were beautiful. I wasn't satisfied with just watching the sunset over the northern prairie. I needed to bring it with me because I knew there was something more to it that I couldn't yet grasp.

The painting at the lake place began to speak to me as I came to these realizations. The flimsy photographs I had been taking were not nearly as beautiful as the humble scene depicted in the family painting—I surmised that I too, should be able to create such a beautiful scene, and only then would I be able to fully grasp this beauty. And that's exactly how my art career began. Decades later my obsession with art would play a pivotal role in helping me kick my anxiety to the curb.

THE SCIENCE

Mode of Expression

Art and art therapy have been used for many years as a viable alternative to treating mental illnesses of differing severity.[21] Doctors and researchers believe that art works to alleviate mental stressors through several mechanisms, one of them being the expression of emotional issues through the art medium.[21] A male cancer survivor in his early twenties may be less likely than a middle-aged female to express himself verbally to friends or a therapist, therefore limiting his ability to vent some of his building anxious or depressive steam. This steam can build up and explode much like a pressure cooker without a vent.

Art has long been a means of expressing feelings that may not easily be put to paper, verse or words: Renoir and his beautiful nudes, JMW Turner and his English seascapes, Monet and the flittering light on his water lilies. Art can be a viable medium of expression for those who find conventional psychotherapy uncomfortable or unnecessary.[22] Ephemeral emotions and feelings are expressed, providing closure and a feeling of relief as negative or strong emotions are exorcised from the body and thoughtfully applied to paper, canvas, or sculpture.

Philosopher Alain de Botton posits that art allows us to probe the depths of our own psyches, therefore teasing out bits of anxiety-inducing pain still deposited deep within us from our cancer experience. He writes:

> *"We are not transparent to ourselves. We have intuitions, suspicions, hunches, vague musings, and strangely mixed emotions, all of which resist simple definition. We have moods, but we don't really know them. Then, from time to time, we encounter works of art that seem to latch on to something we have felt but never recognized clearly before...a fugitive and elusive part of our own thinking, our own experience, is taken up, edited, and returned to us better than it was before, so that we feel, at last, that we know ourselves more clearly."* [23]

It's been said that the art that surrounds someone in their home reflects that person's soul—how much more can that art say about the artist behind it? Often cancer leaves many unanswered and nagging questions that can pester the survivor for years. Trying to explain these feelings to a therapist can be difficult—those who haven't "been there" have extreme difficulty grasping the enormity of cancer's influence on the cancer survivor's present state.

Art, can establish a triadic relationship among the survivor, the image and the art. The art can be the image that symbolizes these buried feelings, and the survivor feels fulfillment when they can produce an image that symbolizes the struggles they went through, in a way that an outsider may find beautiful or tragic. [24]

Control

One of the reasons man makes art comes from a sense of lack of control of one's surroundings. Egotistical man observes a transient, beautiful stream while walking through the woods, and he wishes to capture the beauty of it, wants to control the beauty that it emits so freely, so he returns with a pencil and pad and begins sketching the scene before him. This futile attempt at harnessing nature is a conservative example; think of hydroelectric dams, crop engineering, etc. This need to control one's surroundings is one of the reasons so many of those who have suffered from anxiety or depression naturally gravitate toward art; a semblance of control is placed back into their hands. Those who have beat cancer have been through a situation where their life may have felt out of control. Their health, emotions, and future were in the hands of their doctors.

The ability to put deep-seated and sometimes painful emotions onto paper or canvas puts a level of control back with the survivor.[25] The artist survivor is no longer a prisoner to inner demons when they can put them out in the open. These infectious and cancerous negative feelings left over from cancer are much like black mold. They thrive in environments with little to no sunlight or activity like a dank attic or crawlspace. If left alone, the mold can grow rapidly, but if exposed to the bright light, mold cannot survive.

BENEFITS OF ART THERAPY

A vast amount of literature suggests that art therapy significantly reduces anxiety, depression, and pain and improves the quality of life in survivors.[21,25] Other benefits of art therapy for survivors include:

- Finding an outlet to cope with fear

- Achieve a sense of freedom and self-confidence

- Express buried emotions Art therapy [21]

Many art therapy practitioners have noted counterintuitive benefits from the practice, such as a reduction in tiredness and an energized feeling.[22,26] In my own experience, this increase in energy stems from the veil of mental fatigue being lifted. The constant mental weight of steadfast anxiety or depression can act as tiny weights on the bottom of eyelids, but art appears to act as a lifting spotter—gently helping us curl those weights for a time. Indeed, many cancer centers have taken up art therapy as a viable means of distraction for cancer patients, especially children, who are still blessed with the ability to easily immerse themselves in art.

APPLY IT

If you have opened your eyes while in a department store in the last few years, then you have undoubtedly seen stacks of adult coloring books that have seemingly came out of nowhere. Doodling in coloring books has become a surprisingly huge hit with overworked and stressed-out adults, who can be seen coloring with a box of crayons at restaurants and libraries all around the United States. If you are unsure of where or how to start using art therapy, pick up a coloring book or two at your local store or online.

If you'd rather freestyle, just grab a sketchbook and a pencil and start drawing what you see. If you have kids, finger paint with them.

If you plan on doing any real painting or drawing, I would recommend looking at the work of the masters to get inspired first. If you cannot go to an art museum (which is the best place to study), then many websites host thousands of high-definition images of art from around the world. You can literally see the grains of the canvas on some of the prints, which allows you to study the technique of the artist in minute detail. WikiArt.com is a great starting place.

CHAPTER 10

HEAL YOUR GUT

At some point in your life, you've caught a cold. Maybe that cold lingered for a few weeks—that cough turned from annoying to hacking—and you slid downhill rather than up it. You headed to your nearest clinic looking for an antibiotic fix, knowing that it would make you better, because it has every time before.

After the first few doses, you may have felt sick to your stomach. If you've never wondered why that is, well, you should. The word "antibiotic" literally means opposing life. These drugs are essentially carpet-bombing your intestinal flora, killing anything that lives. While antibiotics often kill the bad bacteria that are making you sick, they also kill the good bacteria. This effect leads to pain reminiscent of a bad batch of heat-lamp shrimp at the all-you-can-eat buffet.

If you went through chemo treatments, you may have been prescribed antibiotics regularly to protect your weakened immune system. I took antibiotics almost weekly for nine months during my chemo stint. You can imagine the amount of damage that can accumulate in your system after prolonged use of these powerful drugs. My monthly chemo treatments left my stomach in a constantly nauseated state. I was either extremely hungry, extremely full and bloated, or just plain sick to my stomach.

But how, you ask, does this affect my anxiety? Well, mounting evidence shows that our "good" stomach bacteria communicate with our brain and influence our health and emotions in a major way. There are roughly five hundred different types of bacteria in our gut, all working together in an almost unimaginably delicate symbiosis. Amazingly, there are ten times more bacteria cells in your gut than cells in your entire body! This delicate balance can be upset, however, and can lead to psychological disturbances.

THE SCIENCE

Studies in mice have shown that an imbalance in gut bacteria can lead to behaviors that indicate anxiety, depression, and autism.[27] In a recent study, mice were dosed with Bacteroides fragilis, a bacterium that protects mice from colitis and leaky gut syndrome. By fixing the gut diseases, the presence of anxiety and depression was almost eliminated.[27]

How exactly does ingesting bacteria help your anxiety though? Researchers have discovered that ingestion of Lactobacillus bacteria regulates GABA production in the brain. GABA is a major inhibitory neurotransmitter in the central nervous system. This chemical produces a feeling of relaxation. Alcohol and yoga produce GABA in large amounts, and we all know how relaxed some boozy downward dog will make you. Healthy gut bacteria also limit cortisol production, which is known as a stress hormone—the opposite of downward dog, like upward cat or something.

APPLY IT

The good news is that you can fix your stomach, slowly but surely. Researchers found that when antibiotics were discontinued in mice, their bacteria returned to normal and brain activity normalized.[29] There is just too little research into gut bacteria in cancer patients to know how long it will take for our bacteria to get back to normal on its own. Your best bet is to speed it up with probiotics.

A study conducted on a group of women found a clear link between probiotics and anxiety reduction. These women were fed yogurt twice a day for a month, because of yogurt's high probiotic content. Brain imaging scans showed a marked improvement in their stress response to anxiety-producing images.[27]

Studies show that certain bacteria strains seem to reduce anxiety and depression more than others. B. Fidobacterium, Lactobacillus and L. Rhamnosus repair the gut quickly and are found in many probiotic capsules found in health food stores. Just be sure to check the label for these strains when shopping.

An even denser concentration of probiotics can be found in certain naturally fermented foods. In the 1930's Dr. Weston Price examined the diets of traditional cultures sheltered from modern diets and industrialized food. These cultures had tremendous vitality and health. The common denominator in all these diets was a daily intake of naturally fermented foods such as sauerkraut, kimchi, and miso. You can get the same benefits and fix your gut by eating these foods daily. When buying these foods, be sure to check that the food wasn't pasteurized, which kills the beneficial bacteria. Look in the refrigerated section of the store. Another reason to use these natural probiotic sources is the cost: a single 4-6 ounce serving of sauerkraut can contain ten trillion bacteria. That means a 16-ounce jar of sauerkraut can have more probiotics than eight to ten bottles of probiotic supplements. You can even make sauerkraut yourself for pennies—all you need is cabbage, salt, and water. Bon appetit!

CHAPTER 11

TRY MUSIC THERAPY

My chemo room is overwhelmingly white and fluorescent. In the adjacent room I can hear a nurse asking a patient's mother for his birthdate, so she can administer some form of chemo. An alarm is blaring down the hall, and figures rush somewhere. My pre-meds are just kicking in; the Benadryl knocks me out and takes the edge off my burgeoning nausea.

After careful consideration, I've decided to try music therapy—the application of music for healing. The research I had done was strong: anxiety and depression can be alleviated with this unorthodox therapy technique.

I'm still worried, however. *A Clockwork Orange* is one of my favorite films. The basic plot is very much dystopian; a young thug named Alex is forced to undergo an experimental therapy called, "the Luvidico Technique." The Technique consists of forcing the patient to watch violent films while being simultaneously injected with drugs that cause intense nausea and pain. The technique is nothing but classical conditioning; Pavlov's dogs were conditioned to salivate when they heard a dinner bell, and Alex was conditioned to feel deathly ill at the merest breath of violence. An unfortunate side effect of the Technique was an accidental aversion to the background score of the films: Beethoven's 9th Symphony. Not only was Alex driven to madness at the mention of violence, but hearing his lovely 9th had the same effect.

I was worried that listening to my favorite concerti would produce similar results. With the risks laid out in front of me, I firmly affixed the Bose headphones to my ears and fired up Vivaldi's Four Seasons. As the vibrant cellos and delicious brass meshed into a beautiful baroque soundscape, my mind slowly drifted away from the earthy chemo room to lush gardens in the ether. It was an escape, and it was everything I needed.

Music is becoming more heavily integrated into medical practices as a peripheral therapy as research proves that its benefits are tangible. I had a port stitched under the skin on my chest to receive chemo fluids early on in my cancer journey. I vividly recall being put under anesthesia: the surgical techs, all in their mid-twenties or early thirties, were listening to some Bob Marley blasting over the speakers in the operating room. Normally the dour seriousness of a medical environment is enough to put me on edge, but the elevated spirits of the techs and the pounding bass seemed to free my anxious mind. The small addition of music made all the difference in how I felt before the procedure.

THE SCIENCE

I learned later that studies backed up these feelings. Music played before procedures can cut anxiety levels, and music therapy has been shown to decrease pain and anxiety during many different types of surgeries associated with breast cancer.[29, 30] In addition, music therapy may also lower the need for drugs associated with pain or anxiety, and studies have shown the effects to be not mere mental reprieve; physical indicators such as heart rate and blood pressure have also been decreased from music therapy.[29, 30] Many medical institutions now staff a music therapist, who "administers" the music in appropriate doses to willing patients. Sounds like a well-paid DJ job to me. These therapists not only cater to cancer patients and survivors, but to people suffering from many different ailments, because music therapy has been proven beneficial for helping alleviate several symptoms across the medical spectrum.[29]

APPLY IT

But what music to listen to? A simple answer is: whatever you like the most, but science will say that classical music has the most benefits. Before turning to music therapy, I had little appreciation for classical music by composers such as Bach, Beethoven, Liszt, or Chopin. I quickly developed an appreciation for this music that continues to this day. I like to listen to Liszt's Bohemian Rhapsody Number Two to get my creative and productive juices flowing at work, and I often turn on a nocturne playlist before bed to relax.

Elizabeth Miles has some good suggestions for starting points in her book, *Tune Your Brain*. She found a set of pieces that will either relax you or uplift you, depending on your goal.

To relax:

- Frederic Chopin: Nocturne No. 1

- To uplift: Joan Ambrosio Dalza: Piva

- George Frederic Handel: Music for the Royal Fireworks, 4th Movement

- Joseph Hayden: Final Movement for the Creation

No matter which musical piece you choose to listen to, it's important to remember to become immersed in the music. Take yourself out of your bed and into the luxurious Vienna Philharmonic, or let Beethoven's strings whisk you away to a tropical island a million miles away from the here and now.

Six months had passed since I had last listened to Vivaldi in my chemo chair. I had a strong aversion to "medical" smells like hand sanitizer or rubbing alcohol, which I associated with chemo. Not wanting to end up like Alex after the Luvidico, I was deathly afraid of listening to classical music again, fearing that at the first downbeat I would become ill.

It took time, but I was feeling especially saucy one night and worked up the nerve to put on my favorite classical playlist. As the first number started, a wide perma-smile ascended onto my face. I couldn't help but remember a scene from the movie where Alex listens to his beloved "Ludwid Van:"

> *"Oh bliss! Bliss and heaven! Oh, it was gorgeousness and gorgeosity made flesh. It was like a bird of rarest-spun heaven metal or like silvery wine flowing in a spaceship, gravity all nonsense now. As I slooshied, I knew such lovely pictures!"*

CHAPTER 12

MEDITATE AND CHANGE YOUR BRAIN

You don't need to throw a kombucha bottle very far to find someone who practices meditation these days. From frazzled executives perched on pillows in their corner suites to working moms stealing a few minutes of me-time, it seems that everyone has discovered what our ancestors knew hundreds of years ago: meditation is awesome.

Meditation is the new "productivity hack," and it has gone mainstream for good reason. Not only can it help you think more clearly and clear the clutter in your mind, but it can also help eliminate anxiety and depression. It's so effective that medical institutions have even started offering it to patients to calm them during or after various procedures. This is backed by reams of medical studies that show how awesome meditation can be for cancer patients and survivors.

THE SCIENCE

A study by the Duke University Medical Center found that meditation eases anxiety and fatigue in women who are undergoing cancer biopsies. [31] A group that participated in guided meditation had much lower levels of anxiety before and after the procedure, and, interestingly, also showed lower levels of overall pain. [31]

In another study, cancer survivors meditated for ninety minutes each week for a period of seven weeks. These survivors saw significant reductions in anxiety levels over survivors who had not meditated. [32]

To examine how powerful meditation can be, check out what it physically does to your brain. In yet another study, people who had never meditated before were tasked with completing eleven hours of guided meditation training. After the eleven hours of training, researchers took MRI scans of their brains. What they found blew their minds: the white matter in the patients' brains had physically improved. The region that improved is involved with control of emotions, thoughts, and behaviors. [33] How cool is that? Your brain really does change from meditation.

APPLY IT

Meditation is one of the first Eastern medical practices to be utilized by conventional Western medical practitioners. But meditation is not just for monks. Most cultures practice some form of meditation. Many Christians practice a form of meditation known as Lectio divina, or "divine reading." Benedictine monks developed this form of meditation in the 3rd century to aid their daily prayer. While many forms of Eastern meditation lead a person to empty their mind or their head, the goal of Lectio divina is to fill one's mind with a verse of scripture—devoting all their attention to studying and internalizing God's word. Many Christians prefer this form of meditation over Eastern forms, which are rooted in Buddhist tradition.

Learning how to meditate can be a daunting task for 21st-century folks. The constant barrage of media and entertainment we are flooded with makes it difficult to "shut off" the parts of our brains that we need to meditate. Be sure to check with your doctor to see if they offer free guided meditation classes, which are extremely helpful for beginners. Here is a quick-start guide to get you off on the right foot:

Basic Meditation

1. *Sit tall. The most common and accessible position for meditation is sitting. Sit on the floor, in a chair, or on a stool. Comfort is key. Now imagine a thread extending from the top of your head, pulling your back, head, and neck up toward the ceiling in a straight line.*

2. *Relax your body. Close your eyes and scan your body, relaxing each body part one at a time. Begin with your toes, ankles, and feet and continue to move up your entire body. Don't forget to relax your shoulders, neck, eyes, and jaw.*

3. *Be still and silent. Now that you are sitting tall and relaxed, take a moment to be still. Just sit, be aware of your surroundings. Don't react or attempt to change anything. Just be aware.*

4. *Breathe. Turn your attention to your breath. Breathe silently yet deeply. Engage your diaphragm and fill your lungs, but do not force your breath. Notice how your breath feels in your nose, throat, and belly as it flows in and out.*

5. *Establish a mantra. A mantra is a sound, word, or phrase that can be repeated throughout your meditation. Mantras can be spiritual, vibrational, and transformative benefits, or they can*

simply provide a point of focus during meditation. They can be spoken aloud or silently to yourself. A simple and easy mantra for beginners is to silently say with each breath, "I am breathing in, I am breathing out." Many Christians focus on words relevant to their faith such as "Jesus" or "charity." As you begin to calm down and focus on your breath or mantra, your mind will calm and become more present. This does not mean that thoughts will cease to arise. As thoughts come to you, simply acknowledge them, set them aside, and return your attention to your breath or mantra. Don't dwell on your thoughts. Some days your mind will be busier than others.

6. *Practice often. Consistency is more important than quantity. Meditating for minutes every day will reward you far greater than meditating for two hours, one day a week.*

7. *Practice everywhere. Most beginners find it easier to meditate in a quiet space at home, but as you become more comfortable, begin exploring new places to practice. Meditating outdoors in nature can be very peaceful, and taking the opportunity to meditate on the bus or in your office chair can be an excellent stress reliever.*

Practice meditation every day if you can. Many find that early morning is the best time to practice, before the kids are up and the bustle of the day distracts. Stick with it, and you'll be a different person in no time.

CHAPTER 13

FREEZE THE ANXIETY OUT

For most people, their shower is their happy place. It's a time when there are no smartphone distractions, no screaming kids, and nothing else to do besides enjoy the soothing stream of water caressing your epidermis. This pleasure can be heightened with the addition of a "shower beer" or the more unconventional "shower wine." A few years ago, a coworker told me that he would often end his showers with five minutes of ice-cold water. I asked him if he was a masochist, and why in the world someone would do that to themselves? He assured me that he received no pleasure from inflicting pain on himself, and that his "Scottish showers," as they are called, offer countless health benefits, not the least of which is anxiety and depression relief. Still unsure of whether the relief of anxiety or depression was worth spoiling the sanctity of the tiled abode, I began to research cold showers and baths.

I examined the relationship my ancestors would have had to cold water in the days before modern conveniences like showers. My great-great-great grandpa in Sweden was a fisherman, like most other men in his village. His typical day was much different from mine. Oscar was constantly exposed, day in and day out, to psychological stressors like wild changes in temperature and exposure to incredible heat and incredible cold. The most extreme temperature fluctuations I am exposed to in a typical day occur during the brief moments when I walk between my heated house and heated car on the way to the office.

Researchers think that depression could stem from a lack of environmental stressors.[34] Extremes in temperature, especially cold extremes, release a flood of feel-good chemicals to the brain. We will get into the how and why later, but the important point to note is that our modern lifestyle of convenience has largely removed us from the extremes of mother nature that man has been subject to for 99 percent of history.

Many cultures value exposure to either pure cold or a combination of hot and cold: the Finns with their saunas, the Turks with their baths, Native Americans with their sweat lodges, and so on and so on. Indian Yogis would travel to the freezing waters of the Himalayan mountains to purify their souls, and Scandinavian-Americans dive into holes cut in ice at "polar plunge" events. Loads of anecdotal evidence suggests that exposing ourselves to extreme cold invigorates or clears the mind, but only recently have we begun to understand the mechanisms that the cold works through to change our minds and bodies.

THE SCIENCE

Early researchers found that unwitting brain stimulation has an antidepressant effect on the brain in almost the same way as electro-shock therapy, which was used extensively to combat depression before modern methods were developed. [34] One study found that regular hydrotherapy (exposure to cold water for thirty seconds or more) could decrease overall tension, reduce fatigue, and elevate mood, while at the same time decreasing pain from rheumatism and asthma. [35] Another study found that depressed patients who took a three-minute shower at sixty-eight degrees Fahrenheit, one to two times a day for two months, had a significant increase in their overall mood and depression levels, while yet another panel found that hydrotherapy was more effective than the common prescription medication Paxil at relieving anxiety and mood instability.[34] Research is piling up in favor of hydrotherapy as an effective treatment (or supplementary treatment) for many nervous disorders.

Exposure to cold water affects those who take the plunge in many ways. For one, the cold water causes blood vessels near the surface of the skin to constrict, pushing blood toward the inner body to conserve heat. This process bathes the brain and vital organs in oxygen and fresh blood, which detoxifies and invigorates.[36] Hydrotherapy is also said to "crowd out" stress hormones like cortisol, allowing the feel-good neurotransmitters to take effect.[35] But hydrotherapy is perhaps most known for controlling systemic inflammation, which is one of the major causes known to us of disease, anxiety, and depression. Regular hydrotherapy calms systemic inflammation and increases levels of beta-endorphin and noradrenaline, which results in a more relaxed and calm mind.[34]

Hydrotherapy also lowers cortisol, which is the body's stress hormone.[36] Once inflammation is lowered and cortisol is brought down to more manageable levels, the balance of neurotransmitters is normalized, and the feel-good transmitter serotonin can effectively relax the nerves.

APPLY IT

Most recommend a minimum of thirty seconds a day of cold water exposure to see real benefits.[34] Start by taking a normal hot shower and apply soap and shampoo per usual, and at the very end turn the faucet all the way to freezing, then count off thirty seconds before jumping into a warm towel. While thirty seconds may be the bare minimum to see results, longer soaks of one to five minutes will only intensify the benefits and more quickly improve your mood. It is important to check with your doctor first if you have any heart problems, are pregnant, or otherwise have medical issues, because not everyone has a heart strong enough to take the bone-jarring cold.

OTHER BENEFITS

Cold exposure offers even more fringe benefits. Cancer survivors are known for their tendency to worry about relapse, so when I found that research suggested that hydrotherapy had anti-tumor effects, I was even happier. Apparently, "daily brief cold stress can increase the number and activity of T lymphocytes and natural 'killer cells,' which are the major effectors of adaptive and innate tumor immunity." [37] In other words, cold showers may be killing or preventing tumors. Another researcher pointed out that daily exposure to cold temperatures could enhance anti-tumor immunity and increase the survival rate of nonlymphoid cancer.[35] And what cancer survivor wouldn't withstand a bit of cold to avoid cancer again?

Hydrotherapy has also gained notoriety lately for its astounding effects on weight loss. Indeed, science has shown that you can burn about four times more fat than the usual rate after only two hours of cold exposure. In Tim Ferriss's book *The 4-Hour Body*, I learned that this is because of something called brown adipose tissue, or BAT, which is a type of fat that actually burns off the bad fat in your body. The cold stimulates this BAT to burn off stores of fat for energy, slimming your beer gut right in time for beach season.

One last benefit of hydrotherapy is improved immunity. Apparently, hydrotherapy increases levels of norepinephrine, which stimulates the immune system to fight off illness. So, forget old wives tales of "catching cold," and crank that faucet over. Just be sure to warn your family beforehand so they don't mistake your screams for something serious.

CHAPTER 14

DRINK MATCHA TEA

Living in such a flat area of the world, it's rare to see a panorama of the surrounding landscape from above. As teenagers we didn't have a romantic "Lookout Pointe" from which we could watch the city lights twinkling below; we had to settle for parking in soybean fields. But from the top floor of the penthouse, I could see dozens of square miles of corn, soybeans, and sugar beets. I soaked up the view as my friend greeted his family.

My friend's family was from Kyoto, Japan, and still honored many of the customs and traditions from the Old Country. I like to think that my family honors Scandinavian traditions in the same manner, but it's hard to brag about customs that include such gems as eating whitefish soaked in lye (the infamous lutefisk) or a movie and TV series that comes painfully close to nailing our "you betcha" English dialect. Herring aside, this particular afternoon I was to take part in one of the oldest customs from Japan, a matcha tea ceremony. I have such strong memories from this experience that even now my scalp tingles as I relive it in my head (it also tingles for different reasons when I remember eating lutefisk).

We take our shoes off and kneel in a circle around his aunt. The ceremony starts with his aunt gently folding and unfolding several small red towels. She delicately places the towels into piles on either side of the small shallow bowl that is used to mix the matcha. The bowl looks handmade, and I later learn that she had made them herself. She pours not-quite boiling water from a black japanned teapot into the bowl, which gently warms the bowl before the tea is added. She carefully picks up on of the folded towels like it was the declaration of independence and dries out the bowl before adding a teaspoon of bright green matcha tea powder. I learned afterward that this weak matcha is called Usu-cha, or "weak tea" in Japanese. A short pour of hot water is followed by brisk whisking with a small bamboo utensil, which transforms the tea into a frothy emerald drink, and my mouth begins to water.

Since this was my first time at a matcha ceremony, I was offered the first drink of the tea. It tasted like a very intense version of the green tea you get from tea bags, but with a much smoother finish and a headier mouthfeel. I grinned politely and passed the tea to my left. Little did I know, but this would be one of the most important tea parties I would ever attend.

After the tea ceremony, my buddy filled me in on the benefits of matcha tea. At the time, matcha wasn't very well-known in my part of the country. It was as exotic as a pomegranate in an igloo at the time. But matcha tea is not a "new" thing; it's been consumed around the world for thousands of years, and is the second most consumed beverage in the world.[38] Buddhist monks have used matcha tea for hundreds of years for its health benefits, which we will get into later. The monks found that the caffeine in the tea stimulated their minds, while another aspect of the tea completely calmed them, allowing the holy men to meditate for hours at a time. Can you imagine meditating for any amount of time after a few shots of expresso? If you don't fall over from the jitters first, you would probably need to hit the bathroom shortly due to the diuretic effects of the mega-dose of caffeine. In the following weeks, I would dive head first into a research-rabbit hole, discovering that matcha tea may be the proverbial fountain of youth.

THE SCIENCE

So about that buzz that the monks would get from it, what's with that? They were chilled out even though they were consuming the same amount of caffeine that you would find in one of today's soft drinks? It turns out there is an amino acid in green tea that acts as a relaxant. This amino acid is called L-theanine, and it is what gives high-quality matcha tea its distinct umami taste.[39] The miracle component is found in the heaviest concentrations in matcha tea, but it is present in smaller amounts within all green and black teas.[40] When you combine caffeine with this amino, think of the resulting cocktail as a vodka Red Bull, only not disgusting and horrible for you. It energizes and relaxes you simultaneously, putting you in the "zone."

L-theanine has been shown to increase your chill factor by two avenues. It stimulates alpha brain waves. Green tea and L-theanine, helps form GABA, which is an important "master" neurotransmitter that controls many other neurotransmitters like dopamine and serotonin.[40] In plain English, it helps increase chemicals in your body that make you feel good, while allowing your brain to go into focus/study/chill mode, which are all good things if you are anxious.[39]

Traditionally it was very labor-intensive and expensive to isolate L-theanine to create supplements and pills for home use. It wasn't until the last twenty years that an affordable and effective L-theanine supplement was invented, dubbed "Suntheanine." Suntheanine is now the most popular form of L-theanine, with studies suggesting that it has beneficial applications including lowering hypertension, increasing learning performance, improving mental acuity, and lowering anxiety levels.[40] All of these are good things in our quest to kick anxiety out of our lives.

Matcha tea is your preferred vehicle to consume L-theanine. There are a couple reasons for this. Remember our meditating monks? They consumed stone-ground, pure matcha and experienced intense meditation from the combination of caffeine and L-theanine. It took a few hundred years, but science has explained why the caffeine and L-theanine working in tandem is more effective than either alone, and why they never got the jitters from the caffeine they consumed in the matcha.

A landmark study tested the effects of L-theanine and L-theanine plus caffeine in a group of individuals. They tested motor skills and other cognitive tasks, and the results were astounding: the group that consumed caffeine and L-theanine together (to equate the effects of matcha tea) had the highest scores in all categories, including simple reaction time, sentence verification accuracy, and numeric working memory reaction time.[38] The study found that the L-theanine inhibited the negative, jittery effects of caffeine, thus allowing the participants to feel the positive effects of caffeine without the negative side effects.[38]

Matcha tea is an all-around awesome thing. It energizes you and relaxes you, and some say it makes you more creative, all while providing a crazy amount of nutrients that are essential to your health. Some studies have shown that matcha lowers bad cholesterol, while more studies point to matcha as being the food with the highest concentration of antioxidants in the entire world. You cannot go wrong with adding this drink to your daily routine, and maybe replacing coffee like many drinkers have, myself included. Unlike some other herbs that relax or calm your mind, matcha and L-theanine don't make you sleepy (kava is bad at this).

So if you're having a stressful day at work and cannot simply zonk out at your desk, have a cup and melt the stress away while keeping the fires burning at the same time. Even if you do decide to use the Suntheanine pills instead of the matcha, rest assured that they are completely safe in the eyes of researchers and government agencies.

CHAPTER 15:

YOUR NEW FAVORITE SPICE

What if I told you there was a magic plant that can relieve depression and bipolar disorder, reduce risk of colon cancer, reduce inflammation, control blood sugar levels, end headaches, and even give you a glowing complexion? No, I don't work at a marijuana dispensary. I'm talking about a spice that the West is now discovering: turmeric. Turmeric, or Curcuma longa, is the signature spice in Indian curry mixes and is what gives table mustard its signature bright yellow color. The powdered root of the turmeric plant has been consumed in Eastern cultures for thousands of years, and there is compelling evidence that turmeric may be the wunderkind of the natural remedy world. Indeed, there are as many recipes for "turmeric milk" on health blogs as there are health blogs.

THE SCIENCE

The compounds that give turmeric its bright yellow color are curcomoids, and they make up 5 percent of the composition of the root. [41] Curcomoids have been proven in scientific studies to affect the expression of more than seven hundred genes in humans, which means that these compounds can positively affect your body in a multitude of ways. [42] Ayurveda (traditional Indian medicine) has documented the therapeutic properties of turmeric and curcumoids for decades, with the most compelling evidence pointing to anti-inflammatory, anti-carcinogenic, antifungal, antibacterial, antidiabetic and antidepressive uses. [41] If you or a loved one is a cancer survivor, even if you don't experience any depression or anxiety, you should know what turmeric can do for you.

There are several mechanisms through which turmeric positively effects your body and mind. It's been shown that "major depression is marked by lower concentrations of both antioxidant enzymes like glutathione peroxidase as well as antioxidants such as glutathione, vitamin E and zinc in blood plasma". [41] Low levels of these antioxidants are indicative of body-wide inflammation, which is a major cause of many chronic health conditions. Turmeric helps to alleviate this inflammation which can affect the brain and lead to depression or anxiety. [41] Curcumin acts as a powerful antioxidant that destroys free radical cells that damage body tissues. [41] While the deliberate use of curcumin as an anti-inflammatory is relatively new in humans, veterinarians have prescribed the compound to horses and dogs for years. [42]

Enter DHA

Researchers have noted that a diet deficient in a chemical called DHA has been correlated with several cognitive disorders, including anxiety and depression.[43] One of the reasons this is such an issue with the typical Western diet is because primary sources of DHA like salmon, sardines, and trout are largely missing at the dinner table.[42] Turmeric has been shown to enhance the synthesis of DHA in humans, meaning the body can better absorb and use the DHA that is consumed.[42]

And the evidence supporting these claims isn't flimsy; turmeric has been cited in more than three hundred scientific papers as a beneficial and safe supplement for humans. Strong evidence suggests that "curcumin can be used with clinical evidence to effectively and safely treat major depressive disorder without suicidal thoughts and psychotic disorders," which are side effects with many prescription depression medications.[42] Professor Glen Schafe notes that "people suffering from PTSD could benefit from a curcumin-enhanced diet."[44]

The most recent and groundbreaking study from UCLA tested the effects of curcumin against Prozac (fluoxetine), a common antidepressant. The study found that the group given curcumin alone saw as much improvement in depressive symptoms as the group given Prozac. [42]

No fear

When we are afraid of something, a connection in the brain has been established to associate a scary stimulus, like a spider, with a fear response. If there is no circuitry in your brain to remind you that you fear spiders, then you simply do not fear spiders. As if turmeric wasn't good enough already, a new study really hoisted the powder onto the collective shoulders of the anxious and depressed around the world: curcumin prevents new fears from being stored in the brain and also removes existing fear memories. [44] Although more studies need to be done, the implications of this discovery could turn the psychology world on its head. Traditionally, cognitive-behavior therapy (CBT) has been the preferred method psychologists and therapists use to remove phobias and fears.

I tested this spice out personally during a particularly oppressive stretch of anxiety in 2013. Bear in mind that this is a personal story than can only be taken as anecdotal evidence; the results are not scientific in the least bit. I was especially busy with my career at the time and was becoming borderline phobic about receiving a call from a customer who tended to raise my anxiety levels through the roof. When he called, it would always be with bad news or a problem, so I became extremely anxious for his almost daily verbal tirades. At the same time, I began to take turmeric for its general anti-cancer properties, fully unaware that turmeric could help erase the fear response. After one week of taking the spice daily, I noticed that I was no longer afraid of the call. With no other changes, I couldn't figure out why I was no longer afraid (why do we always try to pry open the mouth of the gift horse?). The fear response was simply gone.

APPLY IT

Professional surfer Laird Hamilton gets forty-pound crates of turmeric root shipped to his Hawaii home to be juiced and consumed daily. He believes that the root repairs his body and alkalinizes his blood, which increases his energy levels and speeds recovery time. You can make Laird's juice at home, the only thing you may have trouble finding is the raw turmeric root. Check your local health or Asian food store.

Laird Hamilton's Turmeric Juice

- 4 oz freshly juiced turmeric root

- 2 oz raw apple cider vinegar

- 2 tsp raw honey

- 4 drops Bioperine
(black pepper extract, substitute ⅛ tsp black pepper)

- 18oz water

The trick with consuming turmeric and curcumin is to consume it with black pepper or healthy fats, otherwise the body won't absorb the spice well. If you choose to take turmeric or concentrated curcumin capsules, most sources recommend taking between 5-6 grams, or 1 tsp of the powdered spice. Turmeric is very safe, but as always, consult with your doctor first to check for potential drug interactions, and avoid if you are pregnant or breastfeeding.

Since everyone and their brother has a "golden milk" recipe, I'd be a fool not to include my own:

Golden Milk

- 1 cup coconut milk

- 2 cups almond milk

- 2 tsp raw honey

- 1 tsp turmeric powder

- 1 tsp cinnamon

- ¼ tsp ginger

- pinch black pepper

Blend for twenty seconds, then heat in a saucepan for three to five minutes. Serve hot or cold.

CHAPTER 16

PUMP UP THAT TESTOSTERONE

In the midst of the complete chaos of cancer, important details often fall through the cracks. When a cancer patient is given the "all-clear" and joins the exclusive cancer survivor club, there is little fanfare, little celebration, pomp, or circumstance. But inevitably, the newly christened survivor is happy—happy to be done with the painful radiation appointments, the grueling and sickening chemo sessions, and the painfully anxious doctor's office visits. Doctors know this and embrace it, and many leave good enough alone; checking for signs of recurrence is their top priority. Anxiety and depression can happen for various reasons that are sometimes too complex to dive into. It is difficult to find the root cause of the symptoms when dozens of variables have been adjusted in the preceding months.

It is also sometimes counterproductive to warn someone of potential symptoms ahead of time. For example, how often have you told a child that the antibiotic that you are giving her could upset her stomach, only to have her complain of an aching belly minutes after taking the medicine? This effect is universal, and with some people if you tell them that they could potentially have long-term psychological effects from their cancer experience, it plants a seed in their mind that often grows into a nasty little monster.

Low testosterone is one of the unfortunate side effects that often gets overlooked in male cancer survivors. This may be due partly to the fact that "low T" can manifest itself years after treatment ends. Low T usually occurs in males who have had chemotherapy or radiation to the groin area. The links between cancer treatment and low T levels get somewhat blurry. Cancer treatment can have countless effects on body chemistry and psychology, and studies show that the hormonal changes that take place due to chemotherapy can affect short-term and long-term T levels negatively. In a recent study of men with low T, common symptoms included:

- erectile dysfunction

- low libido

- low energy

- sleep disturbances

- depression and anxiety [45]

Half of the men in the study who tested positive for low testosterone had symptoms of depression.[45] These symptoms, combined with debilitating anxiety and depression, equate to a lower quality of life in males suffering from the condition.[46]

Conversely, sixteen trials have shown that men who have taken T supplements have effectively mitigated their depression symptoms without the use of antidepressants.[47] Supplementing with T helped improve:

- Muscular strength

- Fatigue

- Anxiety

- Irritability

- Erectile dysfunction and libido [47]

I first suspected that I might have low T one year after my chemo treatments ended. My anxiety levels were through the roof, my energy levels were low, and good sleep was hard to come by. A commercial on TV came on and asked me if I had "low energy, anxiety, or trouble sleeping?" The ad was selling a drug that older men could inject once a week to increase their testosterone to "feel like a young man again." A lightbulb went off, and I immediately hoped that I had low T; it would be an easy solution for an anxiety problem I couldn't fix, right? The next day I asked my doctor to order me a testosterone blood test, and lo and behold, I was at the very bottom lip of the acceptable range for testosterone levels in men; around 200 ng/l.

So did I pony up and order the shots? Do you know me yet? A bit of internet research told me that the science behind the big pharma T supplements was relatively new, and side effects could be intense. Still wary of any medication after months of chemo, I looked to see if anyone had used alternative techniques to increase their levels. I remembered that in *The 4-Hour Body*, author Tim Ferriss details how he strategically increased his testosterone levels by consuming steak, eggs, and other forms of cholesterol. Cholesterol is the building block of testosterone. A few more steps into the rabbit hole, and I found that another of my favorite authors had written a book specifically for guys looking to naturally increase their T levels. Tucker Max, through a morally-questionable sex act involving x-rays and mountains of radiation coursing through his testes, had nearly destroyed his own T, and he wrote a small book detailing how he got his T back to normal levels.[48]

Max says that he avoided taking T supplements because supplementation eventually knocks the rest of the body's hormones out of whack and is not sustainable. Max believes that five things will help a man naturally and safely increase T levels:

- Food

- Thought and action

- Sex

- Weight lifting

- Sleep

Which he summarizes as simply, "eating bacon, sleeping late, lifting heavy things, and being happy." It sounded legit to me!

Food

Eating strictly unprocessed, natural foods is essential to increasing T levels. Food additives, pesticides, and added chemicals all have a detrimental effect on T levels. Eat plenty of fresh vegetables, good starches such as sweet potatoes and legumes, and lots of good fats like coconut oil, grass-fed butter, and animal fats. Sugars and "white carbs" such as breads, pastas and potatoes should also be avoided, as well as soy-based products and cereals. This eating pattern aligns closely with popular diets such as paleo and slow-carb, as well as eating patterns popularized by Dr. Weston Price.

Up to 40 percent of your daily calorie intake should come from saturated fats such as butter and animal meats. Again, these saturated fats, along with cholesterol, quite literally are the building blocks of testosterone.

Thought and action

While the research is still in its infancy for this category, there is evidence that how we behave effects our hormonal levels as much as hormonal levels affect our behavior. It's like the chicken or the egg conundrum—which one came first? Do guys with high testosterone behave "alpha" because they have high T, or does acting "alpha" cause those guys to have high T? It appears both answers are correct.

My first introduction to this concept came in speech class in high school. Our teacher told us that before a speech, to increase our confidence, we should stand in the classic heavy metal guitarist stance: stand with both feet pointed forward and slowly spread your legs out as far as you can to the sides, keeping the knees locked and legs straight. You should look like the letter "Y" upside-down. This power stance, according to teacher, would change our hormones or something and give us a confidence boost. Sarcastic sixteen-year-olds predictably rolled their eyes at that point, but it was fun to have teacher-regulated air guitar sessions to break up the day.

Max prescribes the "superhero" approach. Think of a superhero you like, and act as if you were him or her. This is like the "what would Jesus do" practice. In my case, I imagined I was Martin Luther, the same Martin Luther who essentially told the Pope, the most powerful man in the world at the time, to stick it. Most of Luther's writings and actions were done in the face of a slow, tortuous death, but fear was not in his vocabulary. In any situation where I felt uneasy or nervous, I imagined and acted like I was Martin Luther—afraid of nothing yet kind and powerful. The idea is that these actions will change your hormone profile, and thus, your behavior. Your T levels will increase with your increasingly alpha-male behavior and actions.

Sex

This is another chicken or the egg argument like the above: those who have more sex have overall higher T levels, and having sex increases T levels simultaneously. Men have higher testosterone levels on the nights when they have had sex than on nights when they haven't. This is a foolproof addition to the plan. Even if having sex doesn't increase your testosterone levels, hey, you had sex?

Weight lifting

Studies have shown that regardless of overall health or wellness levels among a sample of men, "muscular strength is inversely…associated with death from all causes of cancer in men." Essentially, if you're a survivor, you should get strong. Not only do studies prove that it may save your life, but they indicate that it will increase your testosterone levels, thus decreasing anxiety and depression.

The studies specifically cite *strength* as being the key word—not bodybuilding puffy muscles or cardio-derived "fitness," but the ability to lift heavy things up and put them down. By far the best place to start is with compound exercises, which are natural movements that recruit many muscle groups. Examples include bench press, overhead press, squats, deadlift, and pull-ups. One of the most popular free programs available is the 5x5 program. Many fitness gurus recommend 5x5 for both advanced and beginner strength training. A variation of 5x5 has served as the basis of my lifting routine for several years.

Sleep

The last and possibly most important thing you will need to do to increase T levels is get plenty of sleep—eight to nine hours at least. Max recommends sleeping in a completely dark room with absolutely no electronics (or smartphones) nearby. You want to sleep in a cave with nothing in it to distract you.

Deep REM sleep episodes are when the bulk of testosterone is produced, and missing out on this deep sleep will hurt T production long-term.

This is one of those topics that most of my survivor friends have never been exposed to. Too many people experiencing anxiety or depression after cancer, discovering that there is an actionable, measurable thing that they can improve on their own in incredibly motivating. You have blood tests that measure your T levels so you can see when you are successful, and knowing your testosterone has increased has a placebo effect on even the most waifish of gentlemen.

CHAPTER 17

BREATHE LIKE A NAVY SEAL

Due to my excessive absorption of chemotherapy cocktails for many months, my memory of said indulgences is cloudy at best. At one point, I got into a heated argument with my then-girlfriend over what my age was. I legitimately didn't know how old I was. Don't do drugs, kids. Pearl Harbor, the Kennedy assassination, 9/11—we all remember where we were and what we were doing when those landmark events occurred. Likewise, cancer survivors will always remember their first meeting with their oncologist. My first consult was no exception.

At the bright age of twenty-two (or was it twenty-three?) I hadn't met any challenge I couldn't overcome or taken a test I couldn't ace. This machismo exuded from me that day in the office. My doctor, let's call him Dr. Kafka, lobbed one incendiary bomb after another at my parents and I, effectively smothering any ideas we may have had about the casualness of a simple cancer originating in the hand. "You could die. You may have to do chemo. If it has spread to your chest, we have options..."

I kept my composure relatively well. Often the only way to force stoic Midwest Scandinavians from their impassive ways is to present them with a challenge great enough to summon their inner Viking. My upbeat outlook was immediately singled out by Dr. Kafka as one of the most important things that I had going for me in my cancer fight. My age and otherwise great health didn't mean nearly as much to him as my staunch on-to-the-next-one attitude.

Only later would I find out how correct he had been. A popular saying among the go-hard crowd is, "The first fight is in your mind. You must win in your mind before you can win on the court or battlefield."

One way that you can become defeated in your mind is by breathing in a way that limits you neurologically and physically. When you're anxious, it is common to breathe shallowly and from the chest. This breathing style makes your body work harder to capture the same amount of oxygen. This shallow chest breathing has been linked to stimulation of the fight or flight response—a major source of stress and anxiety.

Top athletes and high-performance military men like Navy SEALS utilize breath control to prepare for missions and events.[49] To perform at a high level, these professionals must avoid anxiety at all costs. The anxiety triggers a soldier faces far exceed the stressors that an anxious cancer survivor faces, but the savvy survivor can take a cue from the SEAL or the MMA fighter and breathe in a smarter way.

BOX BREATHING

I first heard about box breathing from a psychologist I was working with at the height of my anxious spell. She showed me the simple breathing exercise, and I immediately had a full-on sensory brain orgasm: my scalp began tingling, spreading down the back of my triceps to the tips of my fingers. An involuntary grin spread across my face as I blissed out in the calming and invigorating exercise. It was something so simple yet so effective. It was the first time I had felt genuinely anxiety-free for months, so I went home to my basement and lifted weights—deadlifts, squats, and bench press, one of my favorite peacetime, feel-good hobbies. The box breathing, coupled with the rush of positive chemicals from the exercise, facilitated my first truly restful night of sleep in weeks.

Box breathing is a "powerful technique to hardwire the brain for clarity and calmness...the effect is instant."[50] The immediate and long-term benefits of box breathing include:

- Reduced performance anxiety

- Control of the arousal response

- Enhanced learning and comprehension [50]

These exceptional benefits are partly due to the doubling of oxygen in the bloodstream, which floods the bloodstream and body with vitality.[50]

How to:

1. Breathe in through your mouth for 5 seconds

2. Hold your breath for 5 seconds

3. Exhale evenly through your nose for 5 seconds

4. Hold your breath for a further 5 seconds

5. Repeat this exercise for 3-10 minutes or longer [49]

RELAXATION BREATHING

When you're panicking or extremely anxious, sometimes it seems impossible to do box breathing; your breathing may be short and fast, and holding your breath would probably put you into the deep end. A fast and safe alternative to box breathing in these situations is relaxation breathing. [49]

How to:

1. Inhale through the mouth for a count of 5, start at the diaphragm and fill up the lungs from bottom-to-top

2. Immediately exhale from top-to-bottom

3. Repeat until anxiety disappears

Relaxation breathing isn't without its share of fringe benefits. This practice has been shown to:

- Increase immune function

- Enhance lung capacity

- Increase energy

- Decrease long-term anxiety [49]

Dr. Kafka instilled the single most important tactical tip in me on our first meeting: control your mind, and the body will follow. As happens with many of the most brilliant teachers, his lesson didn't make sense to me until it did later on. When I was fighting my anxiety, controlling my mind was the theater of war. If the actual battle with cancer is World War II, then the subsequent battle with anxiety is Korea: extremely bloody, unfair, and short. Those who don't take control of their minds through techniques like breathing exercises run the risk of their second battle becoming like the Cold War: long and drawn-out with no clear winner.

No amount of medical help will save you unless you have the heart to fight. If you are reading this and you or a loved one has survived cancer, then you have more fight in you than you realize.

CHAPTER 18

TRY ACUPUNCTURE

Out of all the "tricks" I tried on myself to alleviate the debilitating nausea I was feeling, acupuncture was by far the most effective. I went from experiencing up to fifteen "involuntary regurgitations" per chemo episode to under five. That's a 67 percent decrease in my girlfriend cleaning up my living room carpet.

Acupuncture is defined as the application of stimulation such as needling, moxibustion, cupping, and acupressure on defined sites of the body known as acupuncture points. Acupuncture is used to treat a wide range of illnesses and ailments. Cancer patients use acupuncture for pain management, control of nausea and vomiting, fatigue, hot flashes, neuropathy, and anxiety. Since I had had such great luck using acupuncture for nausea control during treatment, when I started to struggle with anxiety, it was one of the first things that I tried.

The actual process of acupuncture is quite relaxing. When I did it, I would go into a tastefully-decorated and comfortable office, take off my shoes, and enter a dimly lit room where classical music chimed in from the high-end speaker system. No doubt atmosphere plays an important role in the success of this procedure. The acupuncturist inserts tiny needles just under the surface of your skin in the key acupuncture points. Then you chill out in the room for about twenty minutes—long enough for the needles to "cook," as she liked to put it. After leaving the office you can feel an almost dizzying euphoria—a euphoria that's tough to put your finger on, like the feeling of the perfect eighteen-minute nap, or the slight buzz that comes with a good cup of tea or wine. While no one is entirely sure how this works, all I know is that it does work.

At any rate, these acupuncture sessions left me feeling more relaxed and at ease than any other thing going at the time of my anxious spell.

THE SCIENCE

Researchers at Pittsburgh and Temple University conducted one of the most extensive studies on the effects of acupuncture on cancer patients. Specifically, they tested the efficacy of acupuncture on the reduction of pain, anxiety, and fatigue in survivors and cancer patients. No one expected the astounding results.

The study examined "women with advanced breast and ovarian carcinoma." The acupuncture treatment tested was based on Traditional Chinese Medicine (TCM) and was administered by three licensed acupuncturists with an average of seven years' experience. The primary acupuncture points chosen were PC6, L14, ST36, and K13.

Up to fourteen needles were applied to each patient during the session. All the needles were 0.22 x 25mm in length and placed half to three-quarters of an inch below the surface of the skin. Overall, the women in the study experienced impressive relief of anxiety, fatigue, and pain. In total, 63 percent of patients saw a reduction in pain severity, with an average reduction in their symptoms of anxiety as well.

This is a very encouraging study. Not only is acupuncture a

non-invasive procedure, but it is relatively cheap and covered by many insurance plans. Reducing or eliminating anxiety can have more overreaching effects in certain cases. For example, certain forms of breast cancer require survivors to take drugs called aromatase inhibitors (AI's) to treat and prevent breast cancer from reoccurring. These AI's can cause intense joint pain which often leads to anxiety and depression. A study tested the efficacy of a form of acupuncture called electroacupuncture. [51] Electroacupuncture is the same as conventional acupuncture with the addition of electrical pulses in the needles. It is important to reduce this joint pain and anxiety because many breast cancer survivors will quit taking the medicine due to these side effects, which results in increased mortality. The study found that the electroacupuncture reduced fatigue, anxiety, and depression by respectable amounts. Moreover, researchers noted that the positive effects from acupuncture lasted for more than four weeks after treatment.

Again, doctors and researchers aren't exactly sure exactly how acupuncture works on a person's nervous and immune systems, but studies show that it definitely does work. One theory is that acupuncture stimulates nerve centers at the common acupuncture points. This stimulation in turn releases endorphins and serotonin in the blood stream. Serotonin is a natural painkiller and can promote a feeling of well-being.

APPLY IT

Certain medical facilities and institutions now have on-site acupuncturists available to help their patients. This is a relatively new trend, but we can expect this trend to spread as more and more oncologists and doctors realize how effective acupuncture can be. When searching for an acupuncturist, it can be beneficial to ask around for one that has experience working with cancer patients or survivors. A quick internet search should net you some local results.

CHAPTER 19

GIVE YOUR WORRIES AWAY

Let's do a quick exercise. Think back to an instance where you were overwhelmed, swamped, and swimming in a to-do list a mile long. Maybe you're at the office and have five hours' worth of work left to do and it's 4:00 PM on a Friday. There's no way you can get it done in less time, so you're scrambling, trying to find a way to make a miracle happen so you don't have to cancel dinner plans with your family. You work fast, probably too fast, so the quality of your work suffers. You take shortcuts that you normally wouldn't take, and you value your work, so you feel ashamed that you're letting the situation dictate how well you do your job.

Anxiety creeps in. It's tough to read the numbers on the spreadsheet. You feel that panic feeling edging in quickly, out of your peripheral awareness—that part of you that you try to ignore. But ignoring it only makes it stronger. The part of your brain that produces the panic feeling is trying to protect you from something; a threat that your conscious mind cannot see. You can truthfully tell yourself that there is no threat, but that doesn't matter because it's the autopilot part of your brain that won't listen to reason.

You hear a knock on your cubicle wall. Your coworker is dropping by and says she's bored, asks if you need any help.

You feel your tight chest expanding. You breathe deeper. The choking feeling in your throat leaves you. Her offer to help you instantly relieves your anxiety. Almost immediately you think back to how you felt a few moments ago. You look back at yourself from your new calmer position and laugh at how you were anxious for no reason. You think, is this all it takes to rid myself of anxiety: giving some of my problems and worries away?

No doubt you have experienced this feeling before. You are filled with fear and anxiety, and then as quick as the anxiety came, it vanishes. Someone has offered to lift your burden. You can do this anytime you have anxiety for any reason. If you are nervous about a checkup next week or nervous because you have pain in the limb where you had cancer before, you can eliminate this anxiety almost instantaneously. You can do this by writing your worries down, asking a friend to worry for you, or asking God to worry in your place.

ASK A FRIEND TO WORRY FOR YOU

An effective way to study for a test or simply remember something in general is to write it down on paper. This helps your brain catalog and reference the information much better than simply hearing it with your ears and thinking about it. This is because something special happens in your brain before and during the act of putting pen to paper, and it sears the words deeper into your memory.

This process also works the other way around. Let's say you have a list of soup ingredients you need from the grocery store. You could read the recipe before you leave and memorize the ingredients and mentally cross them off as you shop. But this list is stored in a part of your brain that needs a lot of power to hold. If you are constantly repeating these ingredients back to yourself in your head so you don't forget, it will be tougher for your brain to do other tasks, like hold a conversation or perform mental math. But if you write down these items on a shopping list, you free your brain from the strain of juggling these items around. You can apply this principle to remove worries from your brain with great success.

Many writers have "morning pages" that they fill up every day to transfer their fear and frustrations from their heads to paper. Writer Tim Ferriss ritually fills up a few notebook pages every morning to start his day fresh. He writes about things that are bothering him and swears that he never thinks about them again after they leave the tip of his pen. I have a similar practice that I (try to) do every morning as well. I will make a bulleted list in a small notebook and list a current fear that I have. There will usually only be three to five items on the list, and I'll leave a blank line underneath every bullet to make comments. These comments are where I make fun of how insignificant my worries are. For example, under a bullet that reads: "felt a little anxious driving through traffic this morning" I would write: "Ha! You've driven that route 20,000 times and have been fine!"

This helps you re-frame the worries that are now on paper, so you can make light of how ridiculous they really are. Here is an example of one of my real-life worry lists:

Friday, Feb. 24

This morning I am worried about these things:
- guilt over wasting time playing games last night

    - Haha, that's in the past get over it!

- worried I am getting sick

    - Even if you do, you'll survive

- worried about 9:30 meeting

    - You're always worried before them but do great when in them

- worried about this long workday

    - You have been working long days for years, lol

That's all that it takes. Write a few lines on paper, and you're done. You've given yourself permission to not worry about those things for the rest of the day.

You can also tell your worries to a friend to get them off of your plate. Ask a close friend that you can confide in to hear you out, and simply tell them what you are worried about. If they're a close friend, they should gladly take those worries from you. Of course, they won't actually worry for you, but the effect is the same.

You already do this subconsciously without realizing it whenever you vent frustrations or worries in casual conversation. By telling someone what you're worried about, your brain relaxes a bit, because part of that worry has left you and has gone to another person.

Remember back to your childhood when you brought up a concern to your parents. I remember being a little boy and after having watched a movie about a nuclear war, I told my parents I was worried that would happen and we would die. My dad said, "Let me worry about that, son." Of course, that relieved much of my worry immediately, simply because he had made a promise to do something as impossible as transferring a thought from my head to his. But it worked. And it still works.

ASK GOD TO WORRY FOR YOU

I need to preface this by endorsing this as the most helpful part of the book for me. If I were to single out the thing that helped me the most with my anxiety and depression, it's this. My recovery from worry moved at a snail's pace before I started to give my worries to God.

Without getting overly theological, God asks for you to give him your worries. If there is anything bothering you or making you anxious, all you have to do is talk to God, and He will worry for you. For example, I have a friend who was always extremely anxious while driving on a stretch of highway where he was in an accident years ago. As soon as he saw that mile marker, he would grip the steering wheel, and his knuckles would turn as white as a bundle of radishes. This happened every time he drove on this stretch.

One afternoon I was riding with him and noticed him acting strange. Being an anxiety pro myself, I knew that he was dealing with an anxiety episode. Since we were both Christians, I asked him if he wanted to pray over this spot so his anxiety would go away. We both prayed that God would take his anxiety away, so he could drive in peace. We said "amen," and I quickly forgot about it. I got a call from this friend a week later, and he told me that he had driven past that spot five times, and the worry was gone. Simply vanished. I said "Praise the Lord!" and smiled to myself.

I have asked God to take my anxiety away many times, and I still do to this day. I also write down prayers as well, which is even more effective than the prayer alone, in my mind. I'm writing it, which as we already discussed gets the thought out of my head, and I'm asking God to affirm it, further distancing me from the worry. It doesn't take long for my worry to float away.

Now this doesn't work for some people for one reason. The reason is that you don't mean it when you tell God your worries. Let's say you are anxious about your cancer returning, and you ask him to worry about that for you. But, you still allow yourself to worry because you think God didn't hear you. In this case, it's a self-fulfilling prophecy. If you don't truly give it to God, the worry stays with you.

As an anecdotal side note, I should note that the more that I got involved with my church and studying the Bible, the more my anxiety disappeared. It just worked, simply. So if you're not part of a church yet, I recommend going to a service and seeing if it's something that you might like.

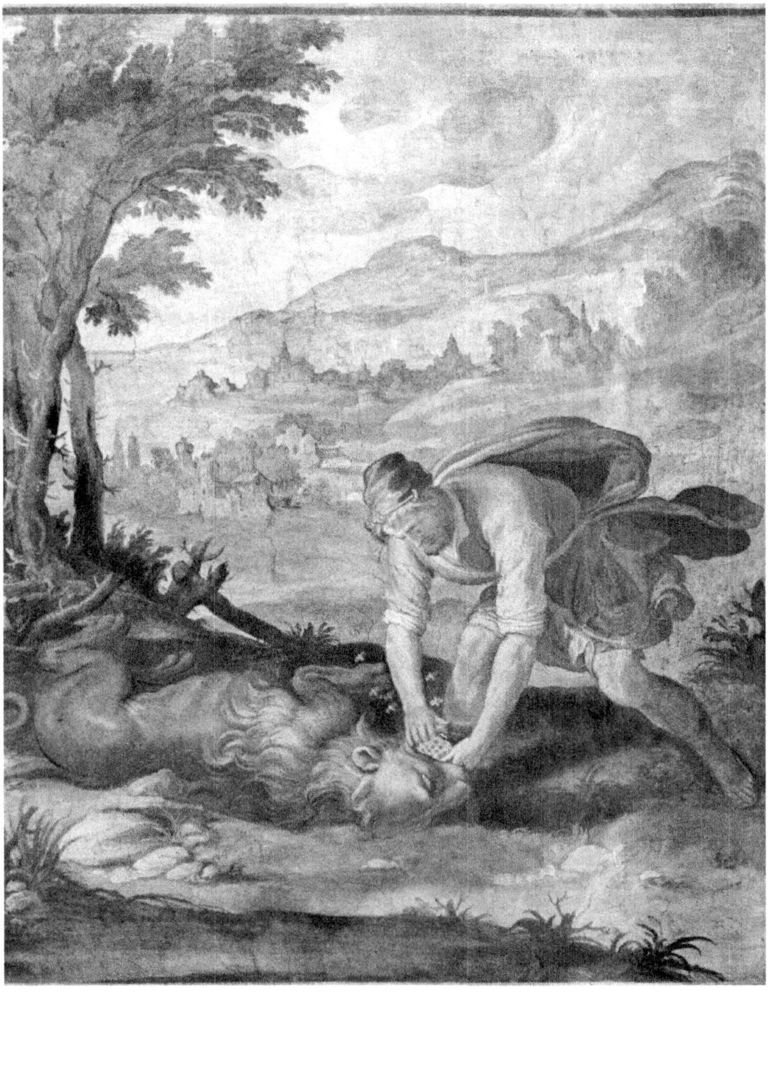

PART III

THE HONEY

Samson killed the lion with his bare hands. Months later, he passed the spot near the orchard where the attack took place. He noticed something strange: hundreds of insects buzzing around the lion's head. Not flies or gnats, but bees. Upon closer inspection, he found a large honeycomb in the lion's mouth, in the very same spot where he delivered his final blow months back. He scooped up a handful of the sweet nectar and laughed to himself.

The force that tried to kill him was now refreshing him with the sweetest food nature can give. The challenge that he faced, and defeated, now rewarded him.

The end of your cancer-anxiety journey will be sweet. You've not only defeated one of the most deadly diseases known to man, but you've also defeated a crippling disease of the mind. While life may dish out unfair and monumental struggles, it always rewards those who persevere, sevenfold.

CHAPTER 20

GROWING FROM CANCER

"Cancer was the best thing that ever happened to me."
—Anonymous survivor

VANCOUVER, BC 2015

Brice Royer's caretaker is sitting next to him in the waiting room of an oncologist's office. His name is Ruso, and he met Royer months before when Royer invited him into his home for a hot meal, not knowing him from Adam at the time. But now, the two are inseparable, like brothers.

Brice had been diagnosed with a rare and deadly form of stomach cancer the year before and fell into a deep depression. A random article in a newspaper changed everything for him: apparently researchers discovered that there was a link between giving and cancer remission. Giving to others and making others smile boosted the immune system and reversed terminal diseases. Some researchers even say that the act of giving scientifically-reduced mortality for everyone. Psychologist Stephanie Brown with the University of Michigan, for example, found that giving reduces mortality by 44 percent .

Reinvigorated with these promising facts and determined to live his last days as selflessly as possible, Brice directed every ounce of his available strength toward helping others. He started by offering meals to people in his neighborhood to foster a sense of community. He even paid a complete stranger's rent for a full year, directly from his own savings. It was from this abundant generosity that Brice met Ruso, and later made him dinner in his home.

Brice recalled, "The tumour actually gave me a gift, because if I didn't have that, I would not have changed my lifestyle, and I would not have appreciated the importance of community and belonging and being surrounded by loving kindness. I probably wouldn't have changed much."

Brice was able to metaphorically take his tumor, a small piece of mutated tissue known for destroying lives, and turn it into a catalyst for improving the lives of those around him.

Brice and Ruso are waiting for results from his latest scans. They will show which direction his cancer tumor has gone—growth or shrinkage. Brice had a migraine that day but was overall optimistic, and it showed in his constant perma-smile that broadcast his love to so many. Brice thinks to himself that maybe the science was wrong, maybe giving was a waste of time and his cancer is still growing. But it couldn't be all for naught—how could giving leave anyone worse off than when they started?

His doctor is younger than most oncologists and sports a healthy stubble that catches many first-time patients off guard; he is often mistaken for one of the youthful interns. The doctor pulls up an MRI image on his computer monitor and points out how Brice's tumor has not only shrunk but has shrunk to a level that could indicate benign cells within the tumor. Brice and Ruso embrace, and a small tear floats down Ruso's cheek.

It's hard to say whether Brice's altruistic activities had an influence on the growth of his tumor, but his story is a great illustration of taking something positive from cancer—taking what should have been the worst thing to happen to you and transforming it into a vehicle for personal growth and selfless giving.

WASHINGTON DC, 1988

The 1988–1989 congressional session was packed with difficult cases, including gender discrimination lawsuits and racially-charged issues. Nothing could prepare Supreme Court Justice Sandra Day O'Connor for the diagnosis her doctors gave her: breast cancer, still in the early stages. The vague language of doctors swam in stark contrast to the concrete rhetoric of lawyers, which irritated her to no end. One thing was perfectly clear, though; Justice O'Connor was going to have a double mastectomy. O'Connor attacked the cancer with the same measured precision that she attacked every threat to come up in her long career in law.

O'Connor recollected what she told herself in the early stages of her struggle: "You better shape up and make a go of this because you're causing a lot of distress for other people."

Astonishingly, Justice O'Connor returned to the bench five days after her double mastectomy, much to the chagrin of her doctors who prescribed bed rest. A grueling schedule of chemotherapy followed. Her son Jon recounted, "She was always thoughtful and on top of things, and it really struck me to see her in a moment so helpless."

The chemotherapy took its toll on the justice. Clerks noted that she seemed, "irritable, frustrated, but swung at every ball." Many patients undergoing chemo take time off from work or resign completely, giving their bodies time to heal. Justice O'Connor would continue to work through her pain and nausea, rarely missing a day on the bench.

POSITIVE CHANGES

Like many of the most successful cancer survivors, O'Connor found the silver lining in her experience. "It made me value each and every day of life more than ever before," she said. Like Brice, O'Connor found a happy and healthy life after beating cancer. They both lived their lives with more vitality and selflessness than before.

One of the reasons they were so happy post-cancer was because they stopped focusing on themselves and their problems and started focusing on others. Viktor Frankl said, "Suffering ceases to be suffering at the moment it finds meaning, such as the meaning of a sacrifice." Brice and O'Connor found meaning in their suffering. Both acknowledged that if they never had cancer, their lives would have been much different after, and not necessarily better.

But many survivors can't find happiness right away. The spirit of giving isn't yet present. Thoughts of themselves and fears of cancer cloud the consciousness. Blaise Pascal's words ring true hundreds of years later: "I have often said that man's unhappiness arises from one thing only, namely that he cannot abide quietly in one room."

The unhappy survivor is afraid of being along with the thoughts of relapse that always surface. The simplest "trick" to get past this is to simply think of others first—be selfless.

Many studies have shown that a healthy minority of cancer survivors are infected with this spirit of giving. They say that cancer woke them up to their materialistic former ways, so they form nonprofit organizations and regularly reach out to new cancer patients who need a mentor. The level of happiness is these survivors is often profoundly greater than those who do not participate in altruistic activities. Here are some of the most common changes survivors experience in the first few years after treatment ends:

The value of time

Maria Shriver, ex-wife of former California Governor Arnold Schwartzenegger, found that she guarded her time much more after beating cancer. She only spends time with people she likes and makes an effort to spend more time overall with the ones she loves and cares about.

Pursuit of lifelong dreams

Finally writing that novel, starting that consulting business, telling your boss to shove it—all of these are common things for survivors to do. They realize that life is too short to do things that they don't want to for forty hours every week. Mental health experts say that survivors seek out more creative, and thus, more meaningful avenues of work or leisure. It's common for a banker to become a poet, while the opposite is rare.

Impatience

A character trait that some may view as negative also pops up in survivors quite often. Brushes with death tend to introduce a sense of urgency into life. Time is more valuable, and time should not be spent on trifling pursuits such as lines at the mall or overtime at the office. The survivors that exhibit this impatience are often the ones who are the most driven by their experience, coincidentally.

CHAPTER 21

TAKING THE FINAL STEP

"To dare is to lose one's footing momentarily. Not to dare is to lose oneself."
—Kierkegaard

What separates winners from losers? Why are some people successful and some aren't? Fear has no hold on the successful ones. They experience fear, but they control it. It doesn't control them. They control fear, harness it, and exploit it.

Fear is the domain of the "dip" Seth Godin coined: the area where the going gets tough, and those who are able to get over the tough stuff reap the rewards. If you're reading this, you're tough. Really tough. You beat a disease that was trying to invade your body and kill you. You put up with the surgeries, the chemo, the radiation, the immunotherapy. The pain, the vomiting. The wigs and the humiliation.

Are you going to let fear keep telling you his lies? You've beat him. He knows that, but maybe you're not convinced yet.

He had you fooled for a bit. He made you anxious, depressed, scared. You felt like you were going crazy. Maybe you were. But you didn't give in. You've applied the tactics from Part 2, and you're seeing results. You're cooler, calmer, and more collected. The tide has shifted, and now you're in charge. Soon, every last bit of anxiety will be eliminated, just like all the cancer was months or years ago.

The only way to go is forward. You're alive, you're going to win, and all you have to do is step forward, one foot at a time, until fear is vanquished from your life forever. Then, you can look back at your victories and notice that you're better off now than before you were diagnosed. You don't take things for granted, and you help others who are going through what you did.

This is the honey—your reward. It is the gratitude you will forever have for every sunrise, every sunset, and every minor trouble in between, and they all will be minor in comparison. Now you just need to use it. If you don't already know how, just listen, and the world will tell you.

BIBLIOGRAPHY

CHAPTER 2: PTSD, THE 1000-YARD STARE

1 French-Rosas, Lindsay. "Improving the Recognition and Treatment of Cancer-related Post-traumatic Stress Disorder." Journal of Psychiatric Practice 17(4) (July 01, 2011): 270-76.

2 "Post-traumatic Stress Disorder (PTSD)." Mayo Clinic. July 06, 2018. Accessed May 05, 2019. https://www.mayoclinic.org/diseases-conditions/post-traumatic-stress-disorder/symptoms-causes/syc-20355967.

3 Yalug, Irem. "Post-traumatic Stress Disorder and Post-traumatic Stress Symptoms in Parents of Children with Cancer: A Review." Neurology, Psychiatry and Brain Research. 17 (2011): 27-31.

CHAPTER 3: CANCER FEARS

4 "Life After Cancer." Cancer.Net. Accessed May 05, 2019. http://www.cancer.net/survivorship/life-after-cancer/coping-fear-recurrence.

5 "Partners Of Cancer Survivors At Risk For Depression." Medical News Today. April 12, 2007. Accessed May 05, 2019. http://www.medicalnewstoday.com/releases/67423.php.

CHAPTER 5: ASMR

6 "ASMR - That's What That Head Tingling Is." The ASMR Lab. Accessed May 05, 2019. http://www.asmrlab.com/.

7 Barratt EL, Davis NJ. 2015. Autonomous Sensory Meridian Response (ASMR): a flow-like mental state. PeerJ 3:e851=https://doi.org/10.7717/peerj.851

CHAPTER 6: NLP

8 "NLP Anchors." The Secret of Mindpower and NLP. Accessed May 05, 2019. https://www.the-secret-of-mindpower-and-nlp.com/nlp-anchors.html.

9 Calming Down: NLP and the Treatment of Anxiety - Transformations NLP. Accessed May 05, 2019. http://www.transformations.net.nz/trancescript/nlp-and-the-treatment-of-anxiety.html.

10 "New Home." Edge NLP. March 15, 2019. Accessed May 05, 2019. https://edgenlp.co.uk/.

11 Winch, Guy. "NLP Experts Speak Out." Psychology Today. Accessed May 05, 2019. http://www.psychologytoday.com/blog/the-squeaky-wheel/201401/nlp-experts-speak-out.

CHAPTER 7: NEUROGENESIS

12 Monje, Michelle, and Jörg Dietrich. "Cognitive Side Effects of Cancer Therapy Demonstrate a Functional Role for Adult Neurogenesis." Behavioural Brain Research 227, no. 2 (2012): 376-79. doi:10.1016/j.bbr.2011.05.012.

13 Rodgers, Shaefali P., Melissa Trevino, Janice A. Zawaski, M. Waleed Gaber, and J. Leigh Leasure. "Neurogenesis, Exercise, and Cognitive Late Effects of Pediatric Radiotherapy." Neural Plasticity2013 (2013): 1-12. doi:10.1155/2013/698528.

14 Dias, G. Pereira, R. Hollywood, M. C. D. N. Bevilaqua, A. C. D. Da Silveira Da Luz, R. Hindges, A. E. Nardi, and S. Thuret. "Consequences of Cancer Treatments on Adult Hippocampal Neurogenesis: Implications for Cognitive Function and Depressive Symptoms." Neuro-Oncology16, no. 4 (2014): 476-92. doi:10.1093/neuonc/not321.

15 Matsuoka, Yutaka. "Clearance of Fear Memory from the Hippocampus through Neurogenesis by Omega-3 Fatty Acids: A Novel Preventive Strategy for Post-traumatic Stress Disorder?" BioPsychoSocial Medicine 5, no. 1 (2011): 3. doi:10.1186/1751-0759-5-3.

16 TED. "You Can Grow New Brain Cells. Here's How | Sandrine Thuret." YouTube. October 30, 2015. Accessed May 05, 2019. https://www.youtube.com/watch?v=B_tjKYvEziI.

CHAPTER 8: EXERCISE

17 Harvard Health Publishing. "Exercising to Relax." Harvard Health. Accessed May 05, 2019. http://www.health.harvard.edu/staying-healthy/exercising-to-relax.

18 Chen, H-M, C-M Tsai, Y-C Wu, K-C Lin, and C-C Lin. "Randomised Controlled Trial on the Effectiveness of Home-based Walking Exercise on Anxiety, Depression and Cancer-related Symptoms in Patients with Lung Cancer." British Journal of Cancer 112, no. 3 (2014): 438-45. doi:10.1038/bjc.2014.612.

19 Segar, M., V. L. Katch, R. Roth, A. Garcia, S. Haslanger, and E. Wilkins. "Aerobic Exercise Reduces Depression And Anxiety, And Increases Self-Esteem Among Breast Cancer Survivors." Medicine & Science in Sports & Exercise 27, no. Supplement (1995). doi:10.1249/00005768-199505001-01188.

CHAPTER 9: ART

20 Lewis, C.S. Mere Christianity. Place of Publication Not Identified: Lightning Source (Tier 1), 2019.

21 "General Cancer Information." Art Therapy | Complementary and Alternative Therapy | Cancer Research UK. November 29, 2018. Accessed May 05, 2019. https://www.cancerresearchuk.org/about-cancer/cancer-in-general/treatment/complementary-alternative-therapies/individual-therapies/art-therapy.

22 Paice, J., N. Nainis, J. Ratner, J. Wirth, and J. Lai. "Relieving Symptoms in Cancer: Innovative Use of Expressive Art Therapy." The Journal of Pain 6, no. 3 (2005). doi:10.1016/j.jpain.2005.01.232.

23 Botton, Alain De. Status Anxiety. London: Penguin, 2014.

24 Boehm, Katja, Holger Cramer, Thomas Staroszynski, and Thomas Ostermann. "Arts Therapies for Anxiety, Depression, and Quality of Life in Breast Cancer Patients: A Systematic Review and Meta-Analysis." Evidence-Based Complementary and Alternative

Medicine 2014 (2014): 1-9. doi:10.1155/2014/103297.

25 "Latest News." American Cancer Society. Accessed May 05, 2019. http://www.cancer.org/cancer/news/creative-arts-beneficial-to-cancer-patients.

26 NorthwesternMed. "Art Therapy Can Reduce Pain and Anxiety in Cancer Patients." EurekAlert! January 01, 2006. Accessed May 05, 2019. http://www.eurekalert.org/pub_releases/2006-01/nmh-atc122705.php.

CHAPTER 10: PROBIOTICS

27 Schmidt, Charles. "Mental Health May Depend on Creatures in the Gut." Scientific American. March 01, 2015. Accessed May 05, 2019. http://www.scientificamerican.com/article/mental-health-may-depend-on-creatures-in-the-gut/.

28 Staff, Science X. "That Anxiety May Be in Your Gut, Not in Your Head." Medical Xpress - Medical Research Advances and Health News. May 17, 2011. Accessed May 05, 2019. http://medicalxpress.com/news/2011-05-anxiety-gut.html.

CHAPTER 11: MUSIC THERAPY

29 "Music Therapy." Susan G. Komen®. Accessed May 05, 2019. http://ww5.komen.org/BreastCancer/Music-Therapy.html.

30 Greco, Alysia. "Effects of Music on Anxiety and Pain in the Diagnosis and Treatment of Patients With Breast Cancer." Pacific University CommonKnowledge, October 8, 2013.

CHAPTER 12: MEDITATION

31 DukeHealth. "Meditation Eases Pain, Anxiety and Fatigue during Breast Cancer Biopsy." EurekAlert! February 04, 2016. Accessed May 05, 2019. http://www.eurekalert.org/pub_releases/2016-02/dumc-mep020116.php.

32 Carlson, Linda E., Zenovia Ursuliak, Eileen Goodey, Maureen Angen, and Michael Speca. "The Effects of a Mindfulness Meditation-based Stress Reduction Program on Mood and Symptoms of Stress in Cancer Outpatients: 6-month Follow-up." Supportive Care in Cancer 9, no. 2 (2001): 112-23. doi:10.1007/s005200000206.

33 Tang, Y.-Y., Q. Lu, X. Geng, E. A. Stein, Y. Yang, and M. I. Posner. "Short-term Meditation Induces White Matter Changes in the Anterior Cingulate." Proceedings of the National Academy of Sciences 107, no. 35 (2010): 15649-5652. doi:10.1073/pnas.1011043107.

CHAPTER 13: COLD WATER THERAPY

34 "Is Cold Water the Ultimate Depression Cure?" Natural Mentor. Accessed May 05, 2019. http://naturalmentor.com/could-cold-water-be-the-ultimate-depression-cure/.

35 Mooventhan, A., and L. Nivethitha. "Scientific Evidence-based Effects of Hydrotherapy on Various Systems of the Body." North American Journal of Medical Sciences 6, no. 5 (2014): 199. doi:10.4103/1947-2714.132935.

36 Bongiorno, Peter. "A Cold Splash–Hydrotherapy for Depression and Anxiety." Psychology Today. Accessed May 05, 2019. http://www.psychologytoday.com/blog/inner-source/201407/cold-splash-hydrotherapy-depression-and-anxiety.

37 Shevchuk, Nikolai A., and Sasa Radoja. "Possible Stimulation of Anti-tumor Immunity Using Repeated Cold Stress: A Hypothesis." Infectious Agents and Cancer 2, no. 1 (2007). doi:10.1186/1750-9378-2-20.

CHAPTER 14: MATCHA TEA

38 Haskell, Crystal F., David O. Kennedy, Anthea L Milne, Keith A. Wesnes, and Andrew B. Scholey. "The Effects of L-theanine, Caffeine and Their Combination on Cognition and Mood." Biological Psychology 77 (2008): 113-22.

39 Juneja, L. "L-theanine—a Unique Amino Acid of Green Tea and Its Relaxation Effect in Humans." Trends in Food Science & Technology10, no. 6-7 (1999): 199-204. doi:10.1016/s0924-2244(99)00044-8.

40 Mason, Russ. "200 Mg of Zen: L-Theanine Boosts Alpha Waves, Promotes Alert Relaxation." Alternative and Complementary Therapies 7, no. 2 (2001): 91-95. doi:10.1089/10762800151125092.

CHAPTER 15: TURMERIC

41 Shruti, and BE Biotech. "10 Benefits of Turmeric In Depression [UPDATED]." Turmeric for Health! April 10, 2019. Accessed May 05, 2019. https://www.turmericforhealth.com/turmeric-benefits/can-turmeric-help-in-depression.

42 "Turmeric - the New Prozac?" Mental Health Food. February 23, 2016. Accessed May 06, 2019. http://mentalhealthfood.net/turmeric-the-new-prozac/.

43 Wu, Aiguo, Emily E. Noble, Ethika Tyagi, Zhe Ying, Yumei Zhuang, and Fernando Gomez-Pinilla. "Curcumin Boosts DHA in the Brain: Implications for the Prevention of Anxiety Disorders." Biochimica Et Biophysica Acta (BBA) - Molecular Basis of Disease 1852, no. 5 (2015): 951-61. doi:10.1016/j.bbadis.2014.12.005.

44 Mailonline, Sophie Freeman For. "Turmeric Prevents Fear Being Stored in the Brain, Scientists Claim." Daily Mail Online. January 19, 2015. Accessed May 06, 2019. http://www.dailymail.co.uk/sciencetech/article-2916435/Could-curry-banish-bad-memories-Turmeric-prevents-fear-stored-brain-scientists-claim.html.

CHAPTER 16: TESTOSTERONE

45 http://www.livescience.com/51453-low-testosterone-men-depression-risk.html

46 Aydogan, Umit, Aydogan Aydogdu, Halil Akbulut, Alper Sonmez, Servet Yuksel, Yalcin Basaran, Ozcan Uzun, Erol Bolu, and Kenan Saglam. "Increased Frequency of Anxiety, Depression, Quality of Life and Sexual Life in Young Hypogonadotropic Hypogonadal Males and Impacts of Testosterone Replacement Therapy on These Conditions." Endocrine Journal 59, no. 12 (2012): 1099-105. doi:10.1507/endocrj.ej12-0134.

47 http://www.naturalhealthadvisory.com/daily/depression-and-anxiety/compelling-new-research-examines-low-testosterone-and-depression/

48 Max, Tucker. How to Naturally Increase Testosterone. Kindle Publishing, 2014.

CHAPTER 17: NAVY SEAL DEEP BREATHING

49 "The Big 4 of Mental Toughness - Part 2." SEALFIT. April 20, 2012. Accessed May 06, 2019. http://sealfit.com/the-big-4-of-mental-toughness-part-2/.

50 Vytautas. "The Instant Stress Relief Strategy Used By SEALS in Combat." High Achiever Diet. August 05, 2016. Accessed May 06, 2019. http://www.highachieverdiet.com/ultimate-stress-relief-strategy-used-by-seals-in-combat-works-within-seconds/.

CHAPTER 18: ACUPUNCTURE

51 "Acupuncture Provides Significant Quality of Life Improvements Among Breast Cancer Patients Taking Drugs to Prevent Recurrence, Penn Study Shows – PR News." – PR News. Accessed May 06, 2019. https://www.pennmedicine.org/news/news-releases/2014/july/acupuncture-provides-significa.